This is a thought-provoking exploration of profound inquiries where Christian faith and human experience intersect, and a must-read for anyone grappling with faith in contemporary life. We're encouraged to wrestle with head-scratching topics, from suffering and evil to the universe's origin, from immigration to AI, all the time engaging in honest, critical reflection. Illuminated with insights from thinkers, scientists, poets and theologians, it's a timely guide for all seeking greater understanding in an increasingly complex world.

—NOEL PURDY, director of research and scholarship, Stranmillis University College

In recent years my son's death has challenged my faith, so reading this book has been timely. It's a book to open your mind, not dictating answers, but gently challenging and leading to an understanding that we have a God of love, whose ultimate purpose is to make all things new. I love the format with short chapters, easy to dip into. Questions included are ideal for small group discussion.

—ROSEY BELL, retired pathologist

This book provides the scaffolding to support conversations that can be transformative for our lives. It unpacks human experience to the full and invites us to explore the conundrums, paradoxes, and dilemmas that emerge. It's a book that will connect people to the wild, unconditional love that sits as the beating heart of the cosmos. With a Leonard Cohen image in mind, may it plunge its readers further into the rays of divine love.

—IAN MITCHELL, Quaker researcher

GW00683731

This is writing of great depth, of immense benefit, a panorama of faith, challengingly described, and providing us with questions to think things through. The author invites us to look further, giving us a framework to do so without imposing answers. Is wrath redemptive? How should we be relating to the LGBTQ+ community? The book invites us not to weaponize God's Word, but to delve the Scriptures and revise the paradigms by which we live.
—IAN TAYLOR, retired medical doctor

This book's fresh thinking on important matters of Christian faith and practice is informed and enriched by wide reading, particularly in literature and the arts. While the book doesn't solve some of my own difficulties with aspects of the God concept, it certainly challenges them. There is much here that deserves a very wide readership, not least the thoughtful consideration of Christian attitudes to LGBTQ issues and to other faiths.
—NORMAN RICHARDSON, honorary fellow in education,
    Stranmillis University College

Fresh Takes
on The Big Questions

Fresh Takes
on The Big Questions

JAMES FERGUSON

RESOURCE *Publications* · Eugene, Oregon

FRESH TAKES ON THE BIG QUESTIONS

Resource Publications
An Imprint of Wipf and Stock Publishers
199 W. 8th Ave., Suite 3
Eugene, OR 97401

www.wipfandstock.com

PAPERBACK ISBN: 979-8-3852-2477-7
HARDCOVER ISBN: 979-8-3852-2478-4
EBOOK ISBN: 979-8-3852-2479-1

version number 09/11/24

For Pamela, Suzanne, Paul, Jay, Rhys, Ruby & Corah
with Faith, Hope, and Love,
and the greatest of these is Love

Contents

Contents

Acknowledgments

IF YOU'RE WRITING A book about life's big questions, how would you begin to acknowledge a lifetime of receiving the wisdom, love and challenge offered by a multitude of people through that time? It would be like writing your autobiography. There's hardly anyone whom you meet and get to know in your lifetime who doesn't, in their own special way, influence your thinking and your approach to the big questions in life. There are so many names that come to my mind as I write this, far too many to list, and if you're reading this, you may be one of those to whom I'm eternally thankful for the words and actions that have influenced my personal responses to the big questions.

My wife Pamela, with her love, care, and wisdom, has been the greatest gift of my life, and I wouldn't think of putting anything in writing without testing it first to get her feedback, and we almost always end up with a shared point of view. Her work and writing as a poet have been inspirational to me and to so many others. I thank too our daughter Suzanne and son Paul, together with the grandchildren, Jay, Rhys, Ruby and Corah, who have done all they can to keep me grounded in our modern, changing world.

I must also mention two couples whose impact on my life and faith has been lifelong. Roy Millar and his wife Rosemary, with their kindness and wisdom, have contributed more than they could ever imagine to the lives and the thinking of Pamela and me. Roy's gifts as a teacher in applying his remarkable Bible understanding have been used widely throughout his life, and you'll find reference to his fascinating commentary on John's gospel, *Come and See: An Invitation to Journey with Jesus and His Beloved Disciple John*, in my bibliography here.

Stephen Critchlow and his wife Rosalind have also had an immense influence on Pamela and me, and their work in various countries and cultures has been characterized by self-sacrificial love for people and for the gospel. Steve's work as a Christian psychiatrist has led to his very helpful insights on mental health in his recent Instant Apostle book, *Mindful of the Light: Practical Help and Spiritual Hope for Mental Health*.

I owe so much to all the wonderful staff and students in Indonesia who shared their insights into the whole range of big questions about life during our time teaching and learning there. I'm thankful too for our short time teaching in Japan, and a much longer time here in Ireland, where so many have made a huge contribution to our lives. A special thanks also to those who have come to live here from many overseas countries, often from hugely challenging situations, who have shared their stories with us, and enriched our thinking about life in a global world.

Abbreviations used in this book

NIV: Holy Bible: New International Version

NRSVue: Holy Bible: New Revised Standard Version Updated Edition

ACDM: Adiabatic Cold Dark Matter

AI: Artificial Intelligence

DNA: Deoxyribonucleic Acid

LGBTQ: Lesbian, Gay, Bisexual, Transgender, Questioning

NASA: National Aeronautics and Space Administration

NHS: National Health Service United Kingdom

UCL: University College London

WHO: World Health Organization

Introductory

I'VE CALLED THIS BOOK *Fresh Takes*, because it's a book looking at a whole range of big questions in life, with the goal of encouraging exploration and discussion. In summing up its purpose, I like the thoughts of John Ciardi, the 20th century American-Italian poet, who wrote that our responses to big questions aren't "bolts to be tightened into place," but "seeds to be planted" that can lead to the growth that comes from creative thinking, all the time leaving more questions, more seeds to help with "greening the landscape."[1]

A recent American survey, as I mention in Chapter One, found the greatest reason for young people turning away from Christian faith was our failure to engage with the hard, challenging, and controversial questions of our modern age. Sometimes being Christian seems to mean living in two different worlds: a world of faith and then the other world with the discoveries of modern science, the arbitrary unfairness of war, poverty, and suffering, and real issues of gender, sexuality and identity. Our goal is to integrate our faith with all of our thoughts and feelings.

The book is arranged under topics, but also with the possibility of dipping in and out of specific questions, as the Table of Contents makes clear. I hope there's enough that takes on the controversial, as well as the most important questions, to challenge and raise discussion opportunities about many areas of contemporary life. I'm also keen to raise discussion of the exciting conclusion summed up so well by Thomas Talbott, that "the ultimate truth about the universe is glorious, not tragic."[2] We sometimes seem to give the impression that the "good news" of the Christian gospel is tragic rather than glorious for so many people in our world.

1. Ciardi, *Manner of Speaking*
2. Parry, *Universal Salvation?* 265

Probing questions were a continual feature of Jesus's life on the streets, and he told wonderful parables about the natural world, because that was the real world in which people lived. Reading the Bible shows us a God who expects us to think, to explore, to struggle with doubts, and to search together for answers, for we're never people who have everything figured out. Faith comes with openness of mind, eagerness to learn, and above all, a love for God's world and all the people with whom we share it.

If you find this book a mix of things that you agree and don't agree with, that's as it should be. I often come back to C. S. Lewis's *Reflections on the Psalms*, where, in Chapter xi, "Scripture," he celebrates the fact that God doesn't provide us with a series of answers to our questions. In Lewis's words, that would be like "trying to bottle a sunbeam." Instead, we have a Bible packed with stories and poems, for "no net . . . less fine than Love will hold the sacred Fish."[3]

3. Lewis, *Reflections on the Psalms*, 92–100

Chapter 1

Big Questions

Life's big questions resist easy explanations, and are usually questions about the purpose and meaning of life and the world we live in. That's why they're always open to fresh perspectives. My aim with this book is to take a wide range of questions that people ask, and provide ideas, suggestions and approaches that have excited me over a lifetime of reading, studying, teaching, and discussing with students in a variety of global cultures in Ireland, the UK, Indonesia and Japan.

The late Chief Rabbi, Jonathan Sachs, has written about how in Judaism, truths about life are most often told in the form of stories, because stories have the advantage of being multi-layered and open-ended.[1] A large part of the Bible is narrative history that focuses on stories of personal, communal and national experiences; stories that provide the depth and challenge we need to give meaning to the complexity of human experience.

C. S. Lewis made a similar point in his chapter on Scripture in his *Reflections on the Psalms*. The Bible uses the whole range of literary genres and literary techniques so that our responses open us to transformation, more than could ever result from a "cut-and-dried, fool-proof, systematic" presentation of what we need to learn. We're provided with a multiplicity of examples of human, lived experience that, as Lewis suggests, enables the human vehicle to become God's life-changing voice.[2]

Around 75 percent of our Christian Bible is made up of narrative and poetry,[3] and that suggests a God who wants us to think, explore, discuss,

1. Sachs, "The Chief Rabbi"
2. Lewis, *Reflections on the Psalms*, 92–100
3. St Francis of Assisi Parish, "Literary Styles"

and work towards conclusions, rather than just be handed propositional answers to our questions. It's not surprising that Jesus found parables of the natural world such a rich means of capturing our imaginations and giving us fresh challenge every time we come back to them.[4]

In a recent survey, Fuller Youth Initiative, an undertaking of Fuller Theological Seminary in Pasadena, California, found that "not having . . . space to ask hard questions is a leading indicator of young people leaving the Christian faith they grew up in."[5] Rachel Held Evans, a well-known American Christian columnist and writer, who died tragically at the age of 37 in 2019 from an allergic reaction to a medication for an infection, wrote about how we make Christian faith difficult, or even beyond consideration, for our present generation, if we avoid facing the hard questions. In her book, *Faith Unraveled: How a Girl Who Knew All the Answers Learned to Ask Questions*, she claimed that doubt and despair begin "not when we start asking God questions, but when, out of fear, we stop."[6] I've called this book *Fresh Takes*, because I want to face the hard questions, and suggest some approaches that go in unexpected directions.

Jonathan Sachs and C. S. Lewis were great examples of celebrating the hard questions, and they certainly didn't have the arrogance of suggesting that they were providing all the answers. They wanted to open up questions for thinking and discussing, and encourage us to reach conclusions. In our present global age, perhaps a new Age of Anxiety, we need that encouragement to journey to faith in a God of love and grace and hope, who shared our human experience in the person of Jesus, and who will walk every step of our path with us.

There are, of course, foundational Christian confessions of faith like the Apostles' and the Nicene Creeds, that sum up in statement form the faith of Christians from the early church to the present day. We benefit hugely from being able to share the truths that unite Christians throughout the world, but that's just the beginning of our lifetime learning process.

Good questions are key. In the learning process, a shared love for the question is a great stimulus to falling in love with an answer. But good answers have to move beyond theory. Our neat theories need to be challenged by the complexities of lived experience. If you're living through the horrors and cruelty of war, or famine, or natural disaster, or poverty, then the big

4. McGrath, *The Open Secret*, 117–26

5. BioLogos, "Asking Questions"

6. Evans, *Faith Unraveled*, 226

questions are questions about survival. For those of us sheltered from day-to-day experience of those realities, our questions and our answers mustn't ignore those facts of life for so many people in our world.

That's why I focus early in the book on chapter 4, "Suffering, Evil and a God of Love." You might ask whether there could be anything fresh to say about the problem of suffering and evil that humanity has been struggling with throughout our history, but connecting it more clearly with how we understand the "universal restoration" that Peter spoke about in Acts 3:21 may help.

In Rachel Held Evans's case, she felt her questions "were seen as liabilities" by the church,[7] because they included issues about our place in the evolutionary process, the age of the earth, poverty, and injustice, and the rights of the LGBTQ community. Part of Evans's return to the church and to faith was the influence of BioLogos, a foundation set up by Francis Collins, leader of the Human Genome Project, and writer of *The Language of God*, where he shares his journey from atheism to faith, and his conviction that science confirms rather than conflicts with faith. The affirmation of BioLogos is that we should never have to choose between science and faith to find answers to our toughest questions.[8] I follow this up in chapter 3, "Modern Science and Christian Faith." Before that, we need to think about the range of signposts that point us not only towards the existence of a God, but also to a God who entered our human life through the incarnation of Jesus Christ, in chapter 2, "Signposts to The Great Story."

The Bible is a library of sixty-six books, but the remarkable thing is that it can be read as one extended story from the creation of the universe in Genesis, through the great drama of the life, death and resurrection of Jesus to redeem the creation that had become alienated from its creator, to God's promise of a new earth in Revelation.[9] In celebrating that wonderful story, the story of every one of us, we need to face up to the hard questions that arise. For example:

- How do we fit nearly fourteen billion years of evolutionary development into the great Bible story?

---

7. Evans, "Fifteen reasons"

8. BioLogos, "God's Word, God's World"

9. See books such as Bartholomew and Goheen's *The Drama of Scripture: Finding Our Place in the Biblical Story*, and Chris Wright's *The Great Story and the Great Commission*.

- How do we make sense of the destructive and cruel side of the evolutionary process, as well as its creative and transformative outcomes?

- Are victims of global warfare, poverty and famine, severe illness and disease, and tragic events and disasters of every kind, just collateral damage in the struggle of life?

- What part of the evolutionary process are we referring to when we talk about a fall into sin and separation from our maker?

- If the creation of a new earth follows God's final judgment, how does judgment fit with the God of love revealed in the Bible, for whom judgment and justice are always connected with mercy, and always have a purposeful and positive outcome?

We won't always agree with each other's answers, but we can keep the open-mindedness that Sachs and Lewis saw as key to hearing God's voice.

Some of my chapters focus on creedal beliefs that are central for Christian faith, such as chapter 5, "The Trinity & the Cross of Christ," and chapter 6, "The Evidence for Jesus's Resurrection." I want the chapter setting out the historical evidence for the resurrection of Jesus to come in the middle of the book, because it's the pivot on which everything else depends. As the apostle Paul wrote, "if Christ has not been raised, our preaching is useless, and so is your faith."[10]

I include biblical challenges to more traditional theology in chapter 7, "The New Creation: Universal Restoration," and chapter 8, "God and the Meaning of Sovereignty." Thinking about how we share the good news of the Christian gospel is explored in chapter 9, "Focus on Christian Mission." In chapter 10, "Contemporary Issues," as well as looking at issues like artificial intelligence, relating to other religions, immigration, and questions of war and peace, I've set out what I think is a biblical call for a welcome, respect, and love for the LGBTQ community.

For theoretical physicist and cosmologist Stephen Hawking, in his final book before his death in 2018, *Brief Answers to the Big Questions*, the really big questions are about science and the universe, to which only a limited number of physicists can suggest answers. Hawking's book provides answers, the majority of them related to the areas in which he excelled, like black holes, the beginnings of life on earth, and shaping the future in the light of scientific advances such as artificial intelligence. Hawking's

10. 1 Cor 15:14

genius earned him the right to claim profound answers to many scientific questions.

Despite that, we need to challenge at least two of Hawking's comments in his book that are less than worthy of his genius. In his first chapter, "Is there a God?" he dismisses the idea of an afterlife in a single sentence because "there's no reliable evidence for it."[11] It seems he hasn't read or considered the historical evidence for Jesus's resurrection, clearly explained in the books written by some of theology's best scholars. I use much of this to sum up the evidence in chapter 6, "The Evidence for Jesus's Resurrection." The most notable study is N. T. Wright's unrivalled two volume investigation, *The Resurrection of the Son of God.*

In his first chapter, Hawking dismisses religion as something people "cling to," because they don't trust or understand science. Again, that view needs to encounter the many thousands of great minds who have celebrated both science and the best of religion as ways to understand the universe we live in. When Einstein wrote that "science without religion is lame; religion without science is blind,"[12] he was making a straightforward claim that we need more than the science of material reality to understand our universe.

It's valid to ask whether there's any value in reasonably short answers to huge questions that have already attracted a host of expert books. In a way, that's the point of this book. I want to open up key questions that still need attention, and using clear, accessible language, offer approaches that might provide us with fresh perspectives.

The book is set out in question form, so that it can be dipped into at the point of any specific question. My responses are also arranged in chapters which become developed units, and these, of course, will give rise to more questions, which is what the process of exploration and understanding is all about. I've also added some further questions at the end of each chapter, so that the book can be used as a resource for group discussion.

Before they came to be known as Christians, the early followers of Jesus were called "followers of the way,"[13] people on a journey through life following Jesus who called himself "the way, the truth and the life."[14] When we look at our lives, or suggest answers to life's biggest questions, it's helpful to stay aware that we haven't arrived yet. American theologian, Frederick

11. Hawking, *Brief Answers* ch.1
12. Einstein, "Science and Religion," 26.
13. Acts 9:2, Acts 22:4, Acts 24:14
14. John 14:6

Buechner, reminds us that "a Christian is one who is on the way . . . and who has at least some dim and half-baked idea of whom to thank."[15] I share what Buechner feels when he speaks self-deprecatingly about himself, but if there's a reason for this book, it's because all of us who know whom to thank, are never able just to settle for our ideas being half-baked. Enjoy the journey.

15. Buechner, *Wishful Thinking*

Chapter 2

Signposts to The Great Story

1. Is there a great story?

2. What signposts point to the great story?

- the natural world

- mathematical signposts

- signposts from science

- creativity and God's image

- music: "the universal language"

- poetry and all the arts

3. So, what is the great story?

1. Is there a great story?

Many people seem to think the Bible is a book of advice and rules about how to live and end up going to heaven when you die. It's a collection of short books and other writings from a long time ago, and they may accept it's got good things to say, especially about the life of Jesus, but, on the whole, they think it has limited relevance to how we live in our present time.

This means we miss the most wonderful thing about the Bible. It's a story, or maybe better, a great drama with a beginning, a middle, and an end, except that the ending is like the greatest of C. S. Lewis's Narnia stories, *The Last Battle*, where Lewis makes clear that Narnia is only the title page, and "Chapter One of the Great Story" is just beginning, with every chapter "better than the one before."[1]

The Bible is a great dramatic story, but is it a true story? Fiction can be true because we learn about life, about relationships, and about the world we live in through it. The Bible story is certainly true in that sense, but it's also true because it's about events that have actually happened, and what those events mean for our lives here and now. Most importantly, every one of us is part of the story, and it's a really hopeful one about us and our lives. Before we look at the great story, let's see some of the signposts that help to make us ready to hear it.

2. What signposts point to the great story?

We might find there are more signposts to life's great story than we think. J. R. R. Tolkien called them "splintered fragments" of "the true light," pointing to "the eternal truth that is with God."[2] C. S. Lewis called them "glimpses" and "echoes" of "the whole cosmic story."[3] Both of them believed there's a great story to discover, and that's why we have Tolkien's Middle-Earth books and Lewis's Narnia stories.

Lewis tells us that we shouldn't be surprised that the imaginations of pagan storytellers provide glimpses into the most exciting part of the great story, the theme of "incarnation, death and rebirth."[4] In his own personal story, *Surprised by Joy*, Lewis's emphasis on desire and longing develops his view of glimpses or echoes provided by God to whet our appetite for what is ultimately true and revealed through the incarnation of Jesus.

William Wordsworth called the signposts "intimations," hints or indications pointing to the "visionary gleam" of a "celestial light," in his poem "Ode: Intimations of Immortality from Recollections of Early Childhood," where he reflects on the struggles in his own life to hold on to the light of that vision.

The word *signpost* also occurs in Seamus Heaney's Nobel Prize winner lecture, "Crediting Poetry."[5] He referred to his poem, "St Kevin and the Blackbird," as a reflection on a story that is both "a signpost and a

1. Lewis, *The Last Battle* 172
2. Carpenter, *J. R. R. Tolkien*, 151
3. Lewis, *Screwtape Proposes a Toast*, 50
4. Lewis, *Screwtape Proposes a Toast*, 50
5. Heaney, *Crediting Poetry*, 20–21

reminder." St Kevin was a 6th century Irish monk at Glendalough in County Wicklow. The story goes that he was praying one day in his tiny monk's cell with his arm stretched out the window space in the stone wall. A blackbird landed on his palm and settled on it to nest. In compassion, Kevin let the bird remain and lay her eggs. After some weeks, the eggs hatched and the new-born birds stayed until they had fledged and flown off. The signpost for Heaney was a story "linked into the network of eternal life," with Kevin's arm a "crossbeam," its Christlike image a reminder of total self-giving and self-sacrificial love.

(i) The natural world

In his book, *The Open Secret: A New Vision for Natural Theology*, Alister McGrath investigates the key issue of natural theology: what we can know about God using our human reason and our observation of the world around us. It's an important question because observation and reason are two fundamental principles of our lifelong learning process.

McGrath takes as his starting point the claim in Psalm 19 that "the heavens are declaring the glory of God."[6] The problem is that what the heavens are declaring can remain just background noise if we have degrees of deafness or difficulty attending to what is being communicated.

We also need to recognize that the word *nature* is not a simple concept and is open to a variety of interpretations, from a mother nature who supplies all kinds of services to humanity, to a wild force "red in tooth and claw," as Tennyson put it in his 1850 poem, "In Memoriam." The more we learn about the natural world, the greater our sense of awe and wonder at its beauty and magnificence, but at the same time, we are part of an evolutionary process that is full of conflict, suffering, and death, as well as being complex, diverse, efficient, cooperative, and progressively transformative.

McGrath's view is that the natural world can provide a signpost pointing to the existence of a transcendent being, but it's the "Christ event," the incarnation of Jesus come to live among us and reveal God in human form, that enables us to understand the natural world, and everything in time and space, as the work of the Christian God. The incarnation is God's way of renewing and transforming not just human nature but the whole created

6. Ps 19:1

universe. Without this, the signposts will only point to "some generalized notion of divinity"[7]

A general understanding of a divine creator based on our observation of the natural world is what Paul writes about in Romans. He tells us that "since the creation of the world God's invisible qualities—his eternal power and divine nature—have been clearly seen."[8] If we put Paul's words into a modern scientific context, the pointers to God's existence might include:

- reliable laws of nature providing a high degree of ordering in the physical universe;

- a degree of uniformity that allows the universe to be studied and makes scientific conclusions possible;

- a remarkable intelligibility in the universe instead of the chaos we might expect;

- conditions that make the development of life possible;

- the vast number of constants precision-tuned to sustain life;

- mathematical designs that apply from the atomic to the galactic;

- an evolutionary process producing intelligent consciousness;

- conscience and awareness of right and wrong;

- objective moral standards and moral laws;

- apprehension of the divine in nature, art and morality;

- apprehension of life's significance;

- a sense of personal responsibility;

- a worldwide religious consciousness.

All of this points to philosopher Antony Flew's conclusion that "intelligence must have been involved."[9]

Clark Pinnock, in his book, *Flame of Love*, writes of how God's "warm breath streams toward humanity with energy and life" through the natural world, with "potentially saving knowledge."[10] McGrath's emphasis is that

---

7. McGrath, *The Open Secret*, 4

8. Rom 1:20

9. Flew, *Has Science Discovered God*

10. Pinnock, *Flame of Love*, 160

potentially saving knowledge only becomes "a radical change" through seeing all of life in the light of the incarnation.[11]

The incarnation enables us to see the revelation of God embedded within nature, exemplified by Jesus's use of the natural world in his seven "I am" sayings in John's gospel,[12] as well as his parables.[13] In the life, death and resurrection of the Messiah, God's message of love became open to the whole of humankind in a new and astonishing way, and the calling of the church is to make this open secret available through word and action.[14]

A crucial goal of education is to help people of all ages learn the language in order to understand what the natural world is telling us, and in that way it can become a signpost pointing us in the direction of our creator. The natural world can provide that glimpse or echo that begins the discovery of the God who became human flesh in the person of Christ.

(ii) Mathematical signposts

The language in which the world is written is first of all a language of mathematics, and this is what makes possible scientific enquiry into everything from the smallest particle to the largest galaxy. Galileo pointed out five hundred years ago that the universe cannot be read until we have learned the language and become familiar with the characters in which it is written, and that is the language of mathematics.[15]

Galileo would be able to make the same claim in our modern world. Physicist, Eugene Wigner, has claimed that the miracle of the appropriateness of the language of mathematics for the formulation of the laws of physics is a wonderful gift that gives us an open door into beginning to understand the universe we inhabit.[16]

When astrophysicist Mario Livio called his book *Is God a Mathematician?* he was searching for an explanation to why mathematics describes reality so well. He's asking the age-old question: whether the principles of maths are invented or discovered. Are they embedded in the universe by the intelligent mind of a creator, or did we construct them ourselves?

11. McGrath, *The Open Secret*, 4
12. John 6:35, 8:12, 10:7, 10:11, 11:25, 14:6, 15:1
13. McGrath, *The Open Secret*, 117–133
14. Ferguson, *Open Secrets,* 68–78
15. Galileo, *Il Saggiatore*, 1623
16. Wigner, "The Unreasonable Effectiveness"

Livio wants to know how "nature knows to obey abstract mathematical symmetries" that apply "from the atomic to the galactic."[17] He presents us with a number of possibilities in a fascinating trip through the history of mathematics, and leaves us with Eugene Wigner's claim that the "the unreasonable effectiveness of mathematics" is "a wonderful gift," even if we don't understand its origin.[18]

The work of students of the natural world has always included discovering that mathematics provides our way of describing the structures of the universe, showing what Mark Tegmark has called the "elegant simplicity and beauty in nature, revealed by mathematical patterns and shapes."[19] It's not surprising that maths points us towards the role of intelligent mind in the origin of the universe.

(iii) Signposts from science

We'll look at science in more detail in the next chapter, so I'll just select some general points here. The quantum world is bringing new challenges to our generation and it's still to maths that we look for answers. When physicist Stephen Barr was asked if quantum theory suggests the existence of God, he answered by suggesting that it has an indirect influence by moving us away from a purely materialist view of the universe.[20]

The astonishing challenges of quantum theory make it harder to accept the claim that everything in our universe is the product of a random process overseen by mindless matter. The award of the 2022 Nobel Prize to three physicists working on quantum entanglement is just one example of our need to be open-minded about what we have always taken to be reality. Quantum entanglement ("spooky action at a distance") means that "when two or more particles link up in a certain way, no matter how far apart they are in space, their states remain linked," so that "any action to one of these particles will invariably impact the others in the entangled system."[21]

Science and religion share a common approach: both investigate the evidence and draw conclusions from it, and we face great problems if we allow science and religion to become disconnected and fail to share the

17. Livio, *Is God a Mathematician?* 6

18. Livio, *Is God a Mathematician?* 224

19. Tegmark, *Our Mathematical Universe*

20. Roa, *Quantum Physics*

21. Sutter, *What is quantum entanglement?*

excitement of all the great discoveries of science. Science should always be teaching us humility and open-mindedness in the face of all we can learn about the universe, and quantum science has added greatly to that.

The map of the oldest light in the universe, taken by the Planck space telescope, has shown us remarkable images of the 'afterglow of creation' nearly 14 billion years ago. The intricate cosmological, chemical, physical, and biological fine-tuning, and the microscopically delicate balances needed to provide the conditions for carbon-based life to exist and develop into the modern consciousness that we call homo sapiens, are so extraordinary that they seem to have needed a universe of this size and age for human life to be able to evolve.

It seems that the creatures God ultimately wants to share in his new heaven and new earth can only develop a consciousness in the likeness of the divine consciousness through a vast process of evolution in a universe as big as this (c.140 billion galaxies), and as old as this (c.13.8 billion years).[22] God has shown us the respect of giving freedom not only to human beings, but also to the universe to evolve within the limits of natural law and within the ultimate purposes of God.

"The heavens are declaring the glory of God" as the Psalmist says,[23] and opening our eyes to the astonishing diversity and complexity of life in our universe can be a prompt to asking questions about its creator, and seeing intelligent mind as the origin of our world.

(iv) Creativity and God's image

The first thing we learn about God in the book of Genesis is that "in the beginning, God created." The first thing we learn about ourselves is that we are made in God's image.[24] God is the first creator and in making us in his image, we are to be co-creators with God. When we speak of being created in the image of God, and therefore being creative people, we're talking about a likeness made visual.

Visual arts have always had a special connection with representing and valuing every aspect of human life. They've also traditionally been associated with the desire to create beauty, and have often been a way of valuing the transcendent beauty of the divine. That was certainly the case

22. Isa 65:17, 66:22, 2 Pet 3:13, Rev 21:1

23. Ps 19:1

24. Genesis 1:26

with the magnificent construction, decoration, and ornamentation of the Jewish temple.[25]

Earlier, in the time of the tabernacle before the temple was built, God was described as gifting with skill and wisdom the garment makers and the craftspeople in ornamental design, to create what was needed for the Jewish priests. Another group of metalworkers, stonecutters, and woodcarvers were "filled with the Spirit of God, with skill, ability, and knowledge in all kinds of crafts, to make artistic designs" for the tabernacle.[26] It's clear that visual arts of all kinds can become pointers to the greatness and glory of God.

We recognize and celebrate those with special talents in creative work, but there is also a need for creativity to be better understood and valued both in education and in all areas of our daily lives and work. It's unhelpful for creativity to be seen as "a distinct category of mental functioning" that has limited overlap with how we often define intelligence.[27] Our view of intelligence often ignores so many of our abilities. If being creative involves "problem-solving by breaking away from usual sequences into different and more productive sequences, giving satisfaction to the self and to others,"[28] then we need to include all kinds of activities that ordinary people do every day. We need to avoid children growing up assuming creativity is something for special people with extraordinary gifts.[29]

Human activities of all kinds involve coming up with solutions to problems, thinking of better ways of doing things and trying them out, and talking about ideas with other people, giving and accepting feedback. Alongside all kinds of creative arts and creative crafts, there are so many creative skills involved in building, repairing and sustaining all areas of our environment, outdoors and indoors.

The most exciting starting point in learning that all of us are creative is our most common daily activity that Ronald Carter calls "the art of common talk . . . the creative artistry in exchanges and interactions that make up so-called everyday spoken language." Carter suggests that we need to realign our thinking and see creative language as "a default condition."[30] If

25. 2 Chron 3 & 4

26. Exod 28:1–5 and 31: 1–11

27. Haensly *Handbook of Creativity*, 53–75

28. Jones, *Creative Learning in Perspective*

29. Ferguson, *Unlocking Creativity*

30. Carter, *Language and Creativity,* 214

we could see "how pervasive is the phenomenon of people being creative,"[31] we might open up a much wider celebration of our creativity, and maybe also, as Joel Clarkson explains, open our eyes to our own involvement in a world of creative artistry that can be another signpost pointing towards a divine creator.[32]

(v) Music: "the universal language"

Henry Wadsworth Longfellow called music "the universal language of mankind" as a result of his European travels in the early 18th century.[33] A 2019 Harvard University study across 315 cultures worldwide found evidence to justify that claim. They found that acoustic features, such as tonality, ornamentation, and tempo, enabled people to have a shared understanding of its psychological impact regardless of cultural background.[34]

Music has been felt in a literal sense as sound waves throughout the whole universe ever since cosmic background radiation began the music of the Big Bang. All of creation is the music of energy waves moving in harmony, proportion, and rhythm. From its inception, "when the morning stars sang together and all the heavenly beings shouted for joy,"[35] to its consummation, when "every creature in heaven and on earth and under the earth and in the sea, and all that is in them" will sing to the Lamb on the throne,[36] creation is musical.

The great Victorian novelist, George Eliot, (Mary Ann Evans), wrote a fascinating, but very long poem published in 1850 called "The Legend of Jubal" in appreciation of Jubal called "the Father of all who play the lyre and the pipe," in the early chapters of Genesis.[37] Eliot pays tribute to the one who expressed "a yearning for some hidden soul of things," and who in the end, knew "the All-creating Presence for his grave." As the Reformed Church in America concluded in their reflection on music in worship,

---

31. Carter, *Language and Creativity*, 81

32. Clarkson, *Three Ways*

33. Longfellow, *Outre-Mer*, 181

34. Asprou, *Music is a universal language*

35. Job 38:7

36. Rev 5:13

37. Gen 4:21

human music-making participates in the music of the cosmos and reflects the order, beauty, and diversity of God's creation.[38]

Together with art and literature, music encourages our journey into recognizing the transcendent, the language that the heavens are declaring, moving discord into harmony, fragmentation into unity, and opening our whole being to the beauty, power, glory, and love that are signposts to the God of love whom we meet in Jesus Christ.

(vi) Poetry and the Arts

Much of what I'm writing here about poetry, and the experience it creates, is also applicable to music, visual art and the arts in general. Poet, theologian, and priest, Malcolm Guite, calls the introduction to his book, *Faith, Hope and Poetry: Theology and the Poetic Imagination*, "Poetry and Transfiguration: Reading for a New Vision." The words *transfiguration* and *vision* give a clue about why reading or hearing great poetry often seems a religious experience.

Part of the reason for that is the function of poetry. As Wittgenstein tells us, "poetry is not used in the language-game of giving information."[39] Poetry is set out differently on the page to prepare us to come with different expectations of it. It asks us as we read to integrate all the resources available to us: thinking deeply, feeling the emotions the thoughts convey, using all our senses to experience what the words and images create, and integrating all of that with the music and the rhythm that the words bring to us.

The transfiguration of Jesus in the gospels was an event when Jesus's divine identity was revealed to three of his disciples, when "his face shone as the sun and his clothes became as white as the light." The disciples were allowed to experience the divine glory of Christ. I recommend reading Malcolm Guite's "A Sonnet on the Transfiguration" where he writes of how "the Love that dances at the heart of things" gives us "a glimpse of how things really are." For Guite, poetry's "image-laden way of knowledge" creates a window "into the mystery that is both in and beyond nature."[40]

Vision is also a word with religious associations. For William Blake, a constant theme is that imagination is the ability to see reality as it really is, beyond what is material. In "Auguries of Innocence," "To see the world

38. Reformed Church in America, *The Theology and Place of Music*

39. Wittgenstein, *Zettel*, 28

40. Guite, *Faith, Hope and Poetry*, 16

in a grain of sand, and a heaven in a wild flower" is the norm of human, poetic vision. The Frontispiece to the engravings in "The Gates of Paradise" tells us: "The sun's light depends on the organ that beholds it." "A fool sees not the same tree as a wise man sees," Blake wrote in one of his letters, for "the tree that moves some to tears of joy is in the eyes of others only a green thing that stands in the way." In his "Vision of the Last Judgment," he wrote: "When the sun rises, do you not see a round disk of fire somewhat like a guinea?" "O no no. I see an innumerable company of the heavenly host crying Holy Holy Holy is the Lord God Almighty."[41]

This means that the impact of poetry is multi-dimensional. It aims to use words in a way that is fresh, and overcomes the dullness and apathy of familiarity, so that our experience of what is said is new and surprising. John Piper, in his article, "God Filled Your Bible with Poems," sums it up well. One reason we love poetry, or maybe even find it too challenging, is because poets often turn to it as the best way to express the complexity of the world we live in and our attempts to make sense of it. Poetry, says Piper, is "verbal resistance to the impenetrability of human experience." For the poet, "this limitation of language does not produce silence; it produces poetry."[42]

As the late Chief Rabbi, Jonathan Sachs, reminded us, we need much more than a simplistic, literalistic, propositional approach to the truths about God and the human condition.[43] "Can we understand the Bible if we don't love poetry?" is the question Matthew Mullins rightly asks in his book *Enjoying the Bible: Literary Approaches to Loving the Scriptures.*[44] In his lecture notes on poetry and the Bible, Mark Wenger finds only seven books in the Bible that have no poetry.[45]

We can take a poem like the great 17th century poet, George Herbert's "Prayer (1)," to illustrate how poetry can create a window so that we see or understand in a completely new way. I'm grateful for Malcolm Guite's detailed and fascinating appreciation of Herbert's use of twenty-seven images to describe prayer in his famous sonnet, and each of them challenges us to see and think about prayer in a fresh way.[46] The poem ends with the lines:

41. Blake, *The Poetical Works*
42. Piper, "God Filled Your Bible"
43. Sachs, "Chief Rabbi"
44. Mullins, *Enjoying the Bible*
45. Wenger, "Poetry and the Bible"
46. Guite, "After Prayer"

"Church-bells beyond the stars heard; the soul's blood;
The land of spices; something understood."[47]

Reflect on what the images bring to mind: all the human situations, calling to worship, celebrate, or mourn, when church-bells ring out. They are our reminder that there is one who entered our human experience in Jesus, who is now our advocate in the presence of the Triune God. Prayer is experienced as a world beyond what our eyes see of material reality. Prayer stirs "the soul's blood," and is the connection with him in whom was life, and that "life is the light of humankind." Think of the multitude of ways needed to keep our blood running through our bodies. Prayer is as essential for the life of our souls as the blood for our bodies. Prayer provides the flavour, the colour, the aroma, the health-giving properties, the enrichment, the mystery of the Orient as "a land of spices."

"Something understood" is a bold, fascinating climax to a poem filled with beautiful and challenging word pictures. What is understood is "something." It's beyond summary, it exceeds Wittgenstein's "language-game of giving information." None of our human language pictures will ever get close to the wonder, the mystery of our relationship with the divine. And "understood" isn't just an intellectual exercise. "Understood" is a final, strong word, effecting an arrival at a new, transfigured state of being.

I use Herbert's poem to illustrate that poetry doesn't set out to be obscure or difficult. It would be very rare to find a poet who doesn't want to be understood, but it challenges us to read and find a window into a new way of seeing. Blake summed up his goal: "If the doors of perception were cleansed, everything would appear to man as it is, infinite. For man has closed himself up, till he sees all things thro' narrow chinks of his cavern."[48] Blake's contemporary, Samuel Taylor Coleridge, describing the poems of the *Lyrical Ballads* that he and Wordsworth published together, saw their purpose as freeing their readers' minds from "the lethargy of custom."[49]

The Bible's celebration of all the arts, of poetry, of music and dancing, of artistry in every type of medium, of imaginative creativity of all kinds, reminds us of the value we should be placing on all the arts in our church life.

47. Herbert, *The Temple*
48. Blake, *The Poetical Works*
49. Watson, *Biographia*

3. So, what is the great story?

This book is really an attempt to wrestle with the questions the great story raises. Questions about God's relationship with the creation, about scientific discovery, about suffering, about evil, and about God's plan to bring about a completely renewed universe, make the great story a story of hope and love that has no rival in human history.

The story begins for us where the Bible begins, for "in the beginning, God created." Was our universe the only creation? We don't know, but it's quite possible there could be other creations. We believe in a God who is a Trinity, a community of perfect love, which means perfect oneness. Why did God create? We meet a God who delights in relationship, and whose requirements are based on two principles. Love the Lord your God with your whole being, and love your neighbor as yourself. Loving God's creation is implicit in those two principles.

That's the beautiful beginning of our story, but we know what happened next. Self-centredness with all its destructive implications took over, and led to episodes of division, of violence, and hatred, so that the most amazing divine plan of rescue was needed. The middle part of the great story is full of unhappiness and suffering, but alongside that, the promise of God to bring blessing to all people in the world.

Yahweh called Abraham and his descendants to be a means of spreading the knowledge of the true God, whose care and concern are not limited to one specific people group, but will be known by all the nations. This promise is developed throughout the Old Testament with the repeated prophecies of the coming of the Messiah, the one sent to bring God's kingdom to both Jews and Gentiles. When Jesus arrived, he announced his messianic calling, quoting Isaiah, as "to proclaim good news to the poor . . . freedom for the prisoners, recovery of sight for the blind, to set the oppressed free, and proclaim the year of the Lord's favor."[50]

We use the word "incarnation" when speaking of Jesus, because God came to live among us as a human being in Jesus. When Philip, one of Jesus's disciples, asked Jesus to show them God the Father, Jesus was very clear. "Do you not know me yet, Philip? If you have seen me, you have already seen God the Father."[51] The great truth of Christianity is that God came to earth in Jesus, and died on the cross to show us what we need to

50. Luke 4:18–19 & Is 61: 1–2
51. John 14:9

know about God. The cross is first of all a language of love and self-sacrifice. Paul explained it like this: "God has shown his great love for us because, when our relationship with God was broken, Christ died for us."[52] The cross is an act of amazing love and a way for us to find forgiveness and our relationship with God to be restored.

The cross then also becomes our model for life. As Joseph Tetlow writes, the cross teaches us "to embrace the world as it really is: full of violence and pain." The cross is a motivation driving the search for peace and for justice. It stops religion becoming "an easy analgesic."[53]

The last part of our story is also the beginning of an even greater one. It begins with the resurrection of Jesus from the dead. We've been looking in this chapter at signposts that point to meaning and purpose in life. The resurrection is the ultimate and supreme signpost, and in chapter 6, "The Evidence for Jesus's Resurrection," I try to do justice to the remarkable amount of evidence that makes the resurrection in our great story completely true. God's power has been demonstrated in victory over death, opening up the same experience for all of humankind in what the Bible calls a "universal restoration." God's wisdom has been shown in allowing evil to do its worst, and using that evil to bring about the greatest good. By taking our place in death, Jesus has rescued us, and set us free to live, free from any condemnation.[54]

Just as exciting as resurrection is the big picture of what Peter told the crowds in his second speech after Pentecost in Acts chapter 3, that there will be a "time of universal restoration that God announced long ago through his holy prophets."[55] It's a promise that transforms our lives here and now, as well as providing a confident hope that justifies Julian of Norwich's beautiful assurance that "all shall be well, . . . and all manner of things shall be well."[56] I try to deal with this in detail in chapter 7, "The New Creation: Universal Restoration."

Further Discussion

1. Are there signposts for you that point to the existence of a divine being?

52. Rom 5:8

53. Tetlow, *The Language of the Cross*

54. Rom 8:1

55. Acts 3:21 (NRSVue)

56. Julian of Norwich, *Revelations of Divine Love* 74–78

2. Are there signposts that go further and point to the Christian gospel of Jesus as God in human form?

3. If you were creating a drama about the Bible's great story in five acts, what might be the main title of each act?

Chapter 3

Modern Science and Christian Faith

1. How do science and religion complement each other?
2. What would contribute to a Christian view of our universe?
   - the origin of the universe
   - consciousness as evidence for a creator God
   - a universe with a purpose
   - evidence of intelligence being involved
   - why a materialist explanation is unsatisfactory
3. Is all of this just speculation?
4. Can we make sense of the evolutionary process?
5. Why has evolution involved waste, destruction, and suffering?
6. What are some key dates in the evolutionary process?
7. Is natural selection the only process at work in evolution?
8. What about the Genesis narrative?
9. What do we mean by the fall of humankind?
10. What is faith?
11. A conclusion: science and faith

1. How do science and religion complement each other?

"Truth is stranger than fiction," wrote Mark Twain.[1] He knew his readers expected the stories in his novels to be probable, or at least credible, otherwise he'd be a writer of a different genre, of fantasy, exploring a world that doesn't exist in reality. If he lived in our day, he'd know that what modern science tells us about the universe we live in, and how it has changed over billions of years, seems even stranger than science fiction.

The Science Council, set up in the UK to provide quality assurance for the sciences, defines science as a way of understanding the world through "a systematic methodology based on evidence."[2] The scientific method is a great tool for helping us understand both the natural and the social world. There will always be mysteries along the way, and modern quantum theory is just one area where we're just at the beginning of understanding our world. We've only begun to make progress on the invisible 95 percent of our universe made up of dark matter and dark energy.

The Cambridge-based Faraday Institute for Science and Religion is named after Michael Faraday, the 19th century scientist who combined a deep Christian faith with an astonishing number of discoveries in physics and chemistry. The Institute uses his name because he's an example of how an intelligent and open-minded approach to both science and religion leads not to conflict, but to dialogue, each learning from the other.

In his book, *Enriching Our Vision of Reality*, theologian Alister McGrath explains the danger of compartmentalizing our minds and fragmenting human experience. We live in one world with all its complexities, and need both science and religion to inform and stimulate each other. We have to deal with what philosopher Karl Popper called "ultimate questions" which shape our lives. Popper recognized that answers to many of our questions require scientific investigation, but many others lie beyond science. They are "riddles of existence" about the meaning of life, and it's foolish to claim that the scientific method alone can lead us to understand all the complexities of our life and human experience.[3]

Science deals with the natural, physical world, and it's widely accepted that our universe began nearly fourteen billion years ago with the Big Bang and has developed through a continual process of biological and geological

1. Twain, "The Pudd'nhead Maxims"
2. Science Council, "Our definition of science"
3. Popper, *Natural Selection*

evolution. That leaves open the question of the origin of the initial hot, dense state that expanded and cooled to allow subatomic particles and later atoms to form, and has been expanding ever since.

We live for a very brief time on a tiny planet, orbiting one of the billions of stars that make up a galaxy that is one of billions of galaxies in the universe. That gives us a huge challenge if we claim that individual humans are a significant part of a bigger story overseen by a loving, divine being. We will need to show that the suffering and loss of any created being can't just be collateral damage in an evolutionary process full of conflict and pain, as well as creativity and transformation.

We also need to show that faith isn't limited to an inner, subjective world, and it's not dependent on fairy stories and wishful thinking, but is based on evidence for an unbreakable relationship with a loving God who's involved in our lives and the world we live in. My starting point is to insist that science and religion share a common approach. Both investigate the evidence and draw conclusions from it. Both embrace our need to seek answers to questions, recognizing how much we still don't know.

2. What would contribute to a Christian view of our universe?

Let me begin by summing up some of the traditional, and very acceptable explanations for a specifically Christian view of the creation and the activity of God in the life of our universe.

(i) The origin of our universe

Theories about the origin of our universe tend to fall into two types. One is a materialist approach, claiming that there is nothing, or at least nothing knowable, outside of material reality. The origin of matter is a mystery, but somehow human consciousness has evolved from sub-atomic particles as a random by-product of a material process. How mindless matter produced all that we call mind remains unexplained.

The second is a theistic approach which believes in a reality beyond our material universe. A Christian view of our finite world depends on an infinite being whom we call God, who is completely self-sustained, but also fully involved in our world.

We know that our universe is at least 13.8 billion years old with the discovery of the oldest light in the universe taken by the Planck space telescope. It shows us the most detailed map ever created of the "afterglow of creation," the cosmic background radiation which is the left-over heat from the Big Bang, the beginning of expansion in which the universe was born.[4] If the universe is the work of God, and humans have some major importance, we need to speculate why God would create a vast and expanding universe that developed for nearly fourteen billion years before human beings appeared.

The big message of the Bible is that God has created free beings who, along with the rest of creation, will ultimately share his new earth, when the heaven of God's presence and the earth of human habitation will be fully integrated. It seems that a human consciousness in the likeness of the divine consciousness could only come into being through a vast process of evolution in a universe as old as this one (c.13.8 billion years).

(ii) Consciousness as evidence for a creator God

A key starting point in the search for evidence for belief in God is the word "consciousness." Consciousness refers to our awareness and experience of ourselves and the world we live in. It includes our thoughts, our feelings, our memories, all our sensory processes, and our subjective mental responses, reactions, and experiences. How consciousness emerged from mindless matter is one of the great unsolved mysteries in neuroscience.

How a kilogram of jelly-like fats and tissues, in which around eighty-six billion nerve cells communicate in quadrillions of connections through chemical and electrical activity, all of it physical and material, can transform into our subjective, conscious awareness and experience remains a mystery. Little has changed since eight neuroscientists wrote in *Human Brain Function* in 2004 that we still have no scientific understanding of the great mystery in the development of life: how consciousness emerges from the physical activity of the brain, and whether consciousness can emerge from non-biological systems.[5]

Some scientists have come to believe that the conundrum of consciousness might even be outside the possibility of the language of science. We don't have the ability to observe consciousness in action, because consciousness is the only thing with which we can do the observing.[6] In his

4. European Space Agency, "Planck reveals"
5. Frackowiak, *Human Brain Function*, 269.
6. John, "Why Science"

recent book, *Being You: A New Science of Consciousness*, Anil Seth seems to recognize that science on its own cannot answer how and why conscious experience arises from physical matter. Science's job is an objective one, to focus on "the properties and nature of conscious experience."[7]

A religious view at least gives us a starting point to finding an explanation for the origin of consciousness. The God who calls himself YHWH in the book of Exodus,[8] a name meaning "I am" and transcribed as Yahweh or Jehovah, uses a name that is the very essence of consciousness.[9] Human consciousness is the result of a long evolutionary process, and the best insight into the mystery of how it has emerged is to see it as an aspect of the ultimate reality that we call God, whose name is "I am." That divine consciousness is reproduced as God's gift at various levels in the human and non-human creation.

That doesn't take us any further in finding a scientific explanation, but it does point to a profound connection between the degrees of consciousness humans and non-human animals possess, and the unlimited consciousness of a God who seeks above all to relate to, communicate with, and live in union with us as persons created in his image. Our human consciousness is the key to the Bible's claim that we are created in the image of God, and live in a universe that is intelligible and made with a purpose. American poet, Emily Dickinson, expressed beautifully how human consciousness is our link with the very being of God in her poem first published in 1896:[10]

> The Brain—is wider than the sky
> For—put them side by side
> The one the other will contain
> With ease—and You—beside
> The Brain—is deeper than the sea
> For—hold them—blue to blue
> The one the other will absorb
> As sponges—buckets—do
> The Brain—is just the weight of God
> For—heft them—pound for pound
> And they will differ—if they do
> As syllable—from Sound

7. Seth, *Being You*

8. Exod 3:14

9. LeFebvre, "I Am Who I Am"

10. Dickinson, *Poems*

Dickinson shares her astonishment at the mystery and miracle of consciousness, the power of the mind to explore, absorb, encompass, and interpret human experience. There's a real sense in which the brain is wider than the sky and deeper than the sea, because the sky and the sea and everything else exist within our consciousness of them. For Dickinson, the metaphor for God's consciousness is "Sound," producing and encompassing all. We, by contrast, deal in "syllables." In other words, we have this inestimable gift of sharing God's image in our creative consciousness, albeit in a vastly more limited way.

American writer, Lee Strobel, shared in a recent tweet the problem that led to his own journey from atheism to belief in God. He found the claim that an aggregation of mindless and thus random, mechanical, unconscious parts has led to life and consciousness is too far-fetched to believe. Belief in a divine creator makes better sense.

NASA's latest Standard Model of Cosmology[11] shows a timeline of the ongoing evolutionary expansion of the universe. Science can't tell us anything about what preceded the Big Bang, but the NASA model suggests a beginning in the sense of a transition from a hot, dense state to an expanding cooler one. What the model cannot suggest is an assumption that the universe may be infinite, because that can only be speculation without evidence. The model shows quantum fluctuations (the spontaneous appearance of energy particles out of the unknown), represented by darkness in the NASA model, and bringing about inflation (massive expansion following the Big Bang). There is much in this model that resonates with a religious understanding of the Big Bang. Forces that come out of the unknown predate the universe and act to set its expansion in motion.

(iii) A universe with a purpose

An evolving universe, as John Polkinghorne & Nicholas Beale write in *Questions of Truth*, is God's gift of love, with creation given the ability to explore its own potential within the parameters set by God. Genesis testifies to this: "Let the earth bring forth living creatures."[12] The evolution of the universe and the development of life are richly creative God-given goals.[13]

---

11. National Aeronautics and Space Administration, ΛCDM *Model of Cosmology*

12. Gen 1:24

13. Polkinghorne, *Questions of Truth*, 56

We live in a universe created with freedom to evolve within the limits of natural laws and of God's overall plans.

The intricate cosmological, chemical, physical, and biological fine-tuning and the microscopically delicate balances needed to allow carbon-based life to exist, and then for that life to develop into the modern consciousness that we call homo sapiens, are so extraordinary that they have needed a universe of this size and age.

That's not to assume that homo sapiens is the be-all and end-all of human evolution. Whatever developments lie ahead, the one thing we know is that all will culminate in God's promise of a new earth where the fullness of God's presence will reign.

(iv) Why a materialist explanation is unsatisfactory

Belief in a divine consciousness is a reasonable explanation for the existence of our universe. A materialist explanation gives us no understanding of how purely physical, material processes could develop into our individually unique experiences of ourselves and the world we live in.

Francis Bacon is often called the father of modern science and the scientific method. In his 1605 book, *The Advancement of Learning*, he was the first writer in English to classify the different forms and types of scientific study. The driving force of scientific study is our human desire for explanation, and, as John Lennox explains, it's sad if that desire for explanation isn't as wide and comprehensive as Bacon's was.[14] For the study of science, Bacon wrote, God has presented us with two books, the book of creation and the book of Scripture. Lennox uses the example of "Aunt Matilda's cake" to describe the limitations of science. There are lots of "what" and "how" questions we can ask the physicist, the chemist and the mathematician to tell us what we need to know about the cake, but the big question we want to ask to satisfy our desire for explanation is why Aunt Matilda has made it. Only Aunt Matilda can tell us that.

For Bacon, the advancement of learning needs both books, the wide-ranging scientific study of the creation and the answers about why the world is here, and why we are here. These are answers that can only be found by asking the creator. For the materialist, there are no explanations to be found. If the Christian Bible claims to be the great story from "in the beginning" in Genesis, to the world that God has planned for us in the

14. Lennox, *God's Undertaker*, 41–44

future in Revelation, at least that big story is worth investigating to satisfy our need for explanation.

The other aspect of our existence that remains unexplained without belief in a creator is what we call the anthropic principle.[15] The anthropic principle is the remarkable number of precise physical conditions that make life on earth possible. A tiny change in any of these conditions would have ruled out life on earth. Astrophysicist Hugh Ross has calculated at least 122 of these unchanging conditions in nature that allow life on earth to exist and thrive.[16] The anthropic principle doesn't prove anything scientifically, but it certainly resonates with belief in a good creator.

Writing about the astonishing degree of fine-tuning needed to produce carbon-based life in our universe, Stephen Hawking and Thomas Hertog suggested in their 2006 article, "Populating the landscape," that we have two choices: an initial state of the universe that is carefully fine-tuned, brought into existence by an outside agency, or else a speculative notion of the generation of many different universes.

Astronomer Bernard Carr defends speculation about a multiverse by calling it one of those ideas that shouldn't be ruled out just because it's outside the normal evidence-based hypotheses of science.[17] You would hope he could recognize that belief in a creator is equally reasonable and with more evidence to justify it. A religious view that sees human consciousness as a God-ordained outworking of the evolutionary process provides a better explanation of the evidence than any other.

(v) Evidence of intelligence being involved

DNA is a molecule containing the unique genetic code of all organisms.[18] It acts as an instructional script, a software programme sitting in the nucleus of the cell. For anyone impressed by numbers, the DNA instructions in a single human cell are more than three billion letters long, and we have around ten trillion cells in our bodies, each of them made up of around ten trillion atoms. It's not unreasonable to suggest that the source of such remarkable complexity might be intelligent mind. Philosopher Antony Flew's journey from atheism to belief was through a conclusion that only

15. Lennox, *God's Undertaker*, 73–77

16. Ross, *The Creator and the Cosmos*

17. Freiberger, "The multiverse"

18. Deoxyribonucleic acid

intelligence could produce such astonishing complexity in the development of life.[19] The conclusion, in the words of theoretical physicist Paul Davies, is that the physical laws of the universe reveal "exceedingly ingenious design."[20]

However, John Polkinghorne and Nicholas Beale are right to see our frequent use of the word "design" as unhelpful in speaking of God's relationship with his creation. Nature's creatures, including ourselves, are not pieces of complex machinery, and children are not "designed" by their parents. As Polkinghorne and Beale write, by creating us in God's own image, we are called to be co-creators of the world we inhabit, which is far beyond being "designed" creatures.[21]

The apostle John described Jesus as the Divine Word who created the world in the beginning.[22] John Lennox sees a remarkable insight in John's use of the metaphor *word*. Given what we now know about the role of DNA in the creation of life, as a database transcribed in alphabetic code,[23] calling Jesus God's life-giving Word has an interesting link with the Jesus "through whom all things were made."

3. Is all of this just speculation?

Religious explanations about the origin of the universe would remain just speculation about a divine creator, if we didn't have the life, death and resurrection of Jesus as events in human history. The resurrection of Jesus is the ultimate evidence for and demonstration of all that we can know about God as the creator and savior of life on earth.

As Karl Barth wrote: "Take away the resurrection, and you've taken away . . . the last hope there is for us on earth."[24] The evidence for Jesus's resurrection is overwhelming when it's clearly explained, and I've put this together in chapter 6 of this book, "The Evidence for Jesus's Resurrection."

19. Flew, *Has Science Discovered God?*
20. Davies, *Superforce*, 243
21. Polkinghorne, *Questions of Truth*, 57
22. John 1:1–3
23. Lennox, *Can Science Explain Everything?*
24. Barth, *Come Holy Spirit*, 299

4. Can we make sense of the evolutionary process?

If some find evolution difficult to reconcile with a biblical Christianity, let me suggest someone whose writings are worth reading. R. J. Berry was Professor of Genetics at University College, London until 2010 and died in 2018. He was a president of Christians in Science and wrote many detailed articles unifying his professional expertise and his deeply held Christian faith. Many of his Christians in Science papers are available online, and his Faraday Paper, "Creation and Evolution, Not Creation or Evolution" is helpful.[25] Berry's books include his 2004 study, *Creation, Evolution and the Bible*, and his 2014 edition of essays by eminent scientists, *Christians and Evolution: Christian Scholars Change Their Minds*.

Let me explain why we can call the foundational meaning of the word "evolution" a fact rather than a theory. Facts tell us what can be shown to be true using overwhelming scientific evidence, but even then, all "facts" remain open to change as more evidence emerges. The process of change in the universe is a fact, while theories are attempts to explain how and why the changes have happened. Almost all scientists are happy to call evolution a fact, while natural selection is one theory to explain it.

C. S. Lewis wrote his essay, "Fern-seed and Elephants," to express his extreme frustration that some theologians at the time he was writing in the 1950s were talking about the gospels as legends or romances, but not histories. As one of the world's leading experts on literary genres, especially in his academic speciality of medieval and renaissance literature, probably no-one in the world knew more than he and his colleague, J. R. R. Tolkien, knew about the distinctions between different genres like myth, fable, saga, romance, allegory, and legend, and how each compared with narrative histories.

Lewis's essay likens theologians who claimed that the New Testament gospels were unreliable as history to people who say they can recognize a tiny fern-seed, when in fact they can't even see an elephant ten yards away in broad daylight![26] As Christians, we shouldn't invite scientists to make the same criticism of us as Lewis made of those theologians. We should recognize the authority of the global science community and not claim we can answer big questions in science through one way of reading the book of Genesis.

---

25. Berry, "Creation and Evolution"
26. Lewis, "Fern-seed and Elephants"

The vast evolutionary process, with genuine freedom for the cosmos and all who live in it, operates within the providential boundaries of what we perceive as natural laws and of God's ensuring that his ultimate purposes are fulfilled. Evolutionary development is a method that God uses to make possible a process of growth that will lead ultimately to living in the fullness of God's presence.

The sending of Jesus into the world as Emmanuel, God with us, brought redemption for the whole cosmos through his death and resurrection, so that every created being can ultimately say that the destination outweighed all the suffering of the journey. St Paul said something similar: "I consider that the sufferings of this present time are not worthy to be compared with the glory that is to be revealed to us."[27]

If there had been a better way for God to achieve his purpose, no doubt God would have used it. Peter's message in his second talk to the crowds after the day of Pentecost drew attention to God's ultimate purpose for the whole created world. Jesus had been with his followers for several days after he rose from the dead, but now he had returned to his Father in heaven. Peter explained, "Jesus must remain in heaven until the time of universal restoration that God announced long ago through his holy prophets."[28] The ultimate goal of universal restoration for the whole cosmos, in a life of perfect consciousness of God in the new earth, means that the conditions of the present will ultimately have been a necessary journey.

5. Why has evolution involved waste, destruction and suffering?

This response to this question can be read together with the discussion of suffering and evil in chapter 4, "Suffering, Evil, and a God of Love," especially questions 5 and 6, on evil and on animal suffering through the evolutionary process.

Waste, destruction and suffering were part of the evolutionary process for hundreds of millions of years before humans arrived on the scene. This means that the conditions of the natural world during that time cannot be an outcome of human sin. The website set up by Christopher Southgate, Professor of Christian Theodicy at Exeter University, and a number of other academics, is called Evolutionary Theodicy,[29] and its aim is to "explore the

27. Rom 8:18
28. Acts 3:21 (NRSVue)
29. A theodicy is a defence of God's goodness, love, power and wisdom in the face

struggle, violence, suffering and extinction in evolutionary biology as a problem for Christian theology."[30]

A starting-point for exploring this struggle is what Canon Bill Vanstone, in his book, *Love's Endeavour, Love's Expense*, writes about the vulnerability that has to come with freedom. The "gift of love" is the freedom that God has given to the cosmos and to its living creatures, and this inevitably opens the door to positive and negative outcomes for humanity and for the natural universe.[31]

While it's true that the evolutionary process has been full of conflict, suffering and death, it has also been complex, diverse, efficient, often cooperative and progressively transformative. Southgate puts this into a positive form in his assertion that death, pain and predation are essential in producing the "range, beauty, complexity and diversity of creatures" that we have in our world. The difficult challenge of Southgate's claim is to accept that "the creation has unfolded as God intended it to unfold."[32] This is just one part of Southgate's comprehensive theodicy that includes God's sharing in every creature's suffering and the inclusion of all creatures in the world to come.[33]

In this way, Southgate answers the question of whether the suffering and death of all creatures are just collateral damage in the wastage of the evolutionary process. It's clear in the Bible that God's restoration of all things in the new creation will involve the whole creation, including all life on earth. I look at that more fully in chapter 7, "The New Creation: Universal Restoration."

The genuine freedom given to us and the world we live in reinforces the biblical picture of a God always active in our lives and our world. Arthur Peacocke's brilliant description of God as the "improvisor of unsurpassed ingenuity"[34] captures the ceaseless involvement of God in all that happens. For further discussion of God's openness to genuine freedom, see my discussion in chapter 8, "God and the Meaning of Sovereignty."

Southgate puts emphasis on the greater good involved in the predatory system. We can see the purpose of death in controlling overpopulation, and

---

of the realities of suffering and evil in the world.

30. https://evolutionarytheodicy.org/

31. Vanstone, *Love's Endeavour*, 62–63

32. Southgate, *Groaning of Creation*, 29–31

33. Southgate, *Groaning of Creation*, 16

34. Peacocke, *Paths from Science*

the need for recycling vital nutrients through dead bodies, enhancing the biodiversity and the ecosystems of life on earth.[35] There is also the adaptive value of things like pain, challenging environments and natural selection.

At least five mass extinctions have changed life on earth.[36] They put a stop to many possibilities but also allowed changes of direction. For example, the extinction of dinosaurs around sixty-six million years ago opened the way for the age of mammals replacing the age of reptiles, an explosive growth of mammal life of which we, as homo sapiens, became beneficiaries. While it's true that extinctions have positive outcomes, such as allowing our own species to emerge, we can never become complacent about their negative impact on all the other species, whose survival and well-being depended on what was lost. Our task now and always is to protect and to preserve.

In our case, as humans created in the image of God, the interplay of positive and negative forces sees more than just providing the conditions for life to develop. It also produces personal, human values that could never exist in a static, 'perfect' universe. We are here to develop spiritual awareness and resources, and that involves the experience of struggle towards growth in love, fortitude, and wisdom. As C. S. Lewis explained in his book, *Mere Christianity*, there would seem to be little purpose in creating a universe without freedom to act, to take responsibility, and to choose to love.[37]

Neil Messer, in his *Zygon: Journal of Religion and Science* article, "Evolution and theodicy: how (not) to do science and theology," examines his problem with Southgate's belief that the suffering experienced by sentient creatures in the evolutionary process was the only way God could bring about the values he wanted in creation. Messer starts with the creation that God saw was good, but God's purposes were disfigured by the presence of evil. Remember, this was a vast age before humans arrived, but there may well have been the same powers of evil that were later to influence humans to rebel and lose their closeness to God. As we saw earlier, freedom for the natural world as well as humanity was always the gift of love, and as Vanstone says, that means vulnerability. Predation and violence entered the

---

35. Rana, "Animal Death"

36. Ordovician c.450 million years ago, Devonian c. 375 mya, Permian c.250 mya, Triassic c.200 mya, Cretaceous c.66 mya.

37. Lewis, *Mere Christianity*, 48

animal world and the evolutionary process, as the outcome of the struggle between good and evil.

Humans, when they come on the scene, are given the pastoral, healing task to look after God's creation. With the "new heaven and new earth," evil will be seen as a power whose days were numbered and will cease to exist in God's new creation.

6. What are some key dates in the evolutionary process?

A timeline for our evolutionary history is and always will be subject to change as more discoveries are made. At the time of writing, modern science tells us that the universe is at least 13.8 billion years old. In the Big Bang, in a minute fraction of a second, the universe expanded from a dense superforce (a singularity), and started the long process of energy changing into matter (and anti-matter). After thousands of years, particles and then atoms emerged, which eventually led to the formation of stars and galaxies, and the universe is still expanding today.

Our Milky Way galaxy appeared c.13.6 billion years ago, our sun and solar system c.4.6 billion years ago, our planet earth c.4.5 billion years ago, and single-cell life c.3.5 billion years ago. Simple animal life formed c.600 million years ago, and mammals c.200 million years ago. There have been five great extinctions of life on earth, c.450, 375, 250, 200 and 66 million years ago, the last being when dinosaurs died out. Scientists estimate that at least 98 percent of all species of plants and animals that ever lived are now extinct.

Modern anthropogeny, the study of human origins, suggests the appearance of the following:

- the order of primate at least 65 million years ago;
- the genus homo c.2.8 million years ago.
- the early species homo habilis, who developed stone tools, disappeared c.1.4 million years ago;
- hunter-gatherer species homo erectus c.1.8 million years ago and disappeared c.110,000 years ago;
- the species homo neanderthalensis c.500,000 years ago and disappeared c.40,000 years ago;

- the fossil record shows that anatomically modern humans, the species homo sapiens, appeared c.300,000 years ago.

Only homo sapiens remains as a distinct homo creature, with language, culture and art.

Some people suggest a special creation in the image of God at some time in the history of homo sapiens. With question 9 below on the fall into sin, I've given a brief summary of R. J. Berry's interesting, detailed argument for an Adam and Eve as a special creation. I can see the appeal in a biblical context of a special creation, but there is also the appeal of the normal scientific view of the emergence of God's image as part of the pattern of evolutionary development from simple to complex life forms, all of it part of God's long-term purposes.

This latter view is expressed by the BioLogos Foundation, founded by Francis Collins, leader of the Human Genome Project, with their aim of demonstrating the integration of science and faith. Writing about how the image of God developed in our human identity, they write that "at BioLogos we believe that God created humans in biological continuity with all life on earth; the distinct cognitive abilities we have were given to us by God through this gradual process."[38]

7. Is natural selection the only process at work in evolution?

We can say with confidence that natural selection explains some aspects of the process by which life has developed, but it has difficulty explaining the emergence of a living cell from non-living material. Seeing natural selection as part of a process that is mindless, motiveless and mechanistic as Dennis Dennett describes the evolutionary process,[39] is a disappointing account of life's complexity and the wealth of genetic innovation and creativity in the world.

To see the vast diversity of forms, capacities and behaviours in the universe as the result of a purposeless, natural process of selection through gradual transformation is an unconvincing explanation. It is too narrow a view of how life has developed. We have a much richer story.

---

38. BioLogos, "How could humans have evolved"
39. Dennett, *Darwin's Dangerous Idea*

8. What about the Genesis narrative?

The late Chief Rabbi, Jonathan Sachs, has written about how in Judaism truths about life are most often told in the form of stories. Stories, both historical narratives and stories written from human imagination, have the great advantage of being multi-layered in their meanings.[40] It is the task of evolutionary and molecular biologists to tell us the scientific report of how life has developed. Genesis is not a science text provided by God to save us the trouble of doing science.

We shouldn't be surprised that stories and poetry make up around three quarters of the Old and New Testaments. Stories provide the depth and challenge we need to give meaning to the complexity of human experience, and that's certainly true of Genesis. Stories have the great advantage of being open-ended and thought-provoking in our desire to make meaning of human life and our relationship with our creator. Sachs saw Genesis as "philosophy in narrative form," a book with "a contemporary feel" about what it is to be human, to have come from "the dust of the earth" and yet to have "the breath of God" within.

A key theme in Genesis is God's gift of choice to humanity, and there we have both the good news and the bad news. The bad news is the speed with which we move from the first turning away from God in chapter 3, to the murder of Abel by his brother in chapter 4, to an earth "full of violence" in chapter 6. But yet, as Sachs emphasizes, it's also a story about how ordinary people can be made extraordinary by "willingness to follow God."

Christians see in the early stories in Genesis the first clues pointing to the great biblical revelation that at the centre of reality is One God, a Trinity of Father, Son and Holy Spirit,[41] a community of divine love in which Three are fully and eternally One. The Word with which the universe is created in Genesis 1 is identified in John's gospel as Jesus, the Word made flesh.[42] The Spirit active in creation is the Spirit outpoured at Pentecost.[43] God's judgment on the serpent is often seen as the first prophecy of the desire of forces of evil to do away with the Messiah, followed by his triumphant resurrection.[44]

40. Sachs, "The Chief Rabbi on Genesis"
41. Swain, "Is the Trinity in Genesis 1?"
42. John 1:14
43. Acts 1:8
44. Gen 3:15

9. What do we mean by the fall of humankind?

The rich story of creation points to God as a creator with very long-term plans over at least the fourteen billion years in which our universe has been evolving. It took most of that time for the conditions for carbon-based life to develop, and for the sort of human consciousness to form that would achieve God's plan to produce created life that would come to share in his new creation, the "new heaven and new earth," which the Bible tells us will follow the end of life on this earth.[45]

The language of the fall of humankind owes much to John Milton's re-working of the Genesis story in *Paradise Lost*. If we are to understand what the Bible tells us about the fall of humankind in the light of modern science, John Polkinghorne suggests that once fully conscious, rational humans appeared in the evolutionary process, this emergent human consciousness must have become aware of the knowledge of good and evil, and recognized the reason for our mortality.[46] Awareness must have developed that our choices of selfishness rather than love derived from wanting to assert our own will over against the good purposes of God. The view of BioLogos mentioned earlier, of a gradual process of development of the image of God in biological continuity with all life on earth, could be extended to include a growing awareness of our human sinfulness.

The book of Genesis shows that we became aware of a different kind of death, a separation from our creator through our moral failures. But Genesis also tells us that we live in a creation that is good. Its goodness lies in its fruitful potential to bring about God's plan and grow to fulfilment, and to us is given the responsibility to love and care for the earth. God could, of course, have created a static and 'perfect' world with no problems for humans to face, but that would have left no possibility of developing, through experience, the qualities like love, compassion, understanding, courage and strength that we need, if we are one day to share in the fullness of divine life in God's new creation.

For those who have difficulty integrating the biblical refences with a process of growth into the image of God, R. J. Berry's 1987 Christians in Science article called "This Cursed Earth: Is the Fall Credible?" is a detailed

---

45. Rev 21:1

46. Polkinghorne, *Questions of Truth*, 68

attempt to justify the idea of Adam and Eve as a special creation at a specific time in the history of humankind.

Using evidence from the background in the Genesis story, Berry argues for the possibility of a historical event around 15000 to 10000 BC in the Neolithic age. A homo sapiens pair were the spiritual founders of humankind when God breathed his image to them, and then to all homo sapiens alive at that time. This, for Berry, was the beginning of homo sapiens as a spiritual being, and was our move from animal life to spiritual humanness in the image of God.

Adam and Eve's failure, rebellion and consequent alienation from God meant a fallen human race, and a fallen earth in the sense of failure in their task to care for the earth as God desired, a failure still evident today. Animal and plant death had always existed throughout evolutionary history, so the result of the fall was spiritual death. We have been given the opportunity to resume our God-given role through Christ, though creation will continue to "groan" until God's completion of the new heaven and new earth. Berry saw his article as an attempt to do what philosopher, Francis Bacon, in his 1605 *The Advancement of Learning*, desired—to bring together God's two books, the book of creation and the book of Scripture.

Ultimately, the whole evolutionary process needs to be understood in the light of creation's destiny now and beyond death in a redeemed universe. The goal is a transformed world free from both moral evil and the physical characteristics of death, destruction and suffering, all of this made possible by the self-sacrifice of Jesus on the cross. The focus of the gospel, meantime, remains on the transformation of our present world, here and now.

10. What is faith?

In his *Church Dogmatics*, Karl Barth provides a definition of faith that is both memorable and profound. Faith, he writes, "is the gift of the meeting in which we become free to hear the word of grace which God has spoken in Jesus Christ" and the outcome of hearing is that we hold fully and exclusively "to his promise and guidance."[47]

Barth's definition suggests that when we are open to communication with God, then the gift of a meeting with a God who is always wanting to communicate with us takes place, and faith is the outcome. This gift of a

47. Barth, *Dogmatics in Outline*

meeting between the divine and the human enables an integrated understanding of ourselves and the world we live in, and leads to the confidence and trust we can place in the God revealed in Jesus Christ.

Christian faith is committed to openness to all that God reveals to us in the Bible, and recognizes that there are many other ways in which God communicates with us. In all of this, faith is committed to critical thinking based on honest, intensive investigation of the past and the present. That's why Paul writes so clearly about his belief in the resurrection of Jesus as a factual, historical event. "If Christ has not been raised, then our preaching is useless and so is our faith."[48] I try to do justice to the huge amount of evidence that leads to a rational basis for belief in chapter 6, "The Evidence for Jesus's Resurrection."

A conclusion: science and faith

Both science and religion search for truth, and the truth about ourselves and the world we live in is big enough to require the insights of both disciplines. Both science and faith believe in approaching questions using rational thought and belief in objective truth. Faith must not be deprived of the discoveries of science, and science needs the wonderful framework for understanding reality that Christianity provides. Albert Einstein chose his words carefully and convincingly when he claimed that "science without religion is lame; religion without science is blind."[49] In our responses to the big questions, we need to welcome and be excited by all that science and the Christian faith offer us as ways to understand ourselves, our world, and the meaning of our existence.

Further Discussion

1. Do we need both science and religion to understand ourselves and our universe?

2. Do you find enough in a materialist explanation to account for our existence?

3. Are there aspects of modern scientific explanations that you find hard to reconcile with Christian faith?

48. 1 Cor 15:14
49. Einstein, *Science, Philosophy and Religion,* ch.13

4. Why might God use an evolutionary process over billions of years in creating the universe?

Chapter 4

Suffering, Evil, and a God of Love

1. What is the problem of suffering?

2. Have suffering and death always been part of the evolutionary process?

3. Can we believe in a God who loves us when the world is full of suffering?

4. Can we find any solutions to the problem of suffering?

   - the soul-making explanation

   - our human responsibility

   - God on the cross

   - all able to say that the glory to come will eclipse the evil and the suffering

5. What about the suffering of non-human animals?

6. Can we explain the existence of evil?

7. Why does God allow disasters?

8. Do miracles happen, and if so, why not more often?

9. Where can we find unshakable hope for the world?

1. What is the problem of suffering?

The problem is easily stated. Why is life on earth so full of suffering if there's a God who loves us and is all-powerful? Does God not want to prevent suffering, or is he not able to prevent it? Dostoevsky's great novel completed in 1880 just before his death, *The Brothers Karamazov*, struggles with this problem. Ivan is a young student who tries to believe in a God who is good, but he faces a dilemma: "If the sufferings of children go to make up the sum of suffering needed for the purchase of truth . . . the entire truth is not worth such a price."[1]

The existence and the extent of suffering in the world are the biggest problems we have to face if we believe in a God of unlimited power who has unfailing love for all he has made. The Bible faces up to the problem, but always in the context of lived experience, rather than as a philosophical question with a theoretical answer.

I can see the integrity in that approach. We're shown respect, and given the ability to wrestle with big issues, rather than being given an answer book with everything worked out in advance. We see the responses of the characters in the book of Job, the huge range of responses in the Psalms and in the writings of the prophets, and in New Testament responses to all forms of persecution, and above all, in the experience and response of Jesus.

In our own time, few writers have wrestled with the problem more profoundly than Holocaust survivor and Nobel Prize winner, Elie Wiesel. He has written more than fifty books, including his harrowing record of his experiences as a 15-year-old boy in Auschwitz and Buchenwald in *Night*, and remarkable novels like *The Testament*, *The Gates of the Forest*, and *All Rivers Run to the Sea*. His play, *The Trial of God*, was set in a fictional Eastern European setting after a violent Jewish pogrom, and is based on Wiesel's witness of a real-life debate between Jewish rabbis in Auschwitz, putting God on trial for what they were suffering.

Wiesel's play was the inspiration for Frank Cottrell-Boyce's 2008 television drama set in Auschwitz and called *God on Trial*. The Auschwitz prisoners hold a debate, after which they vote and find God guilty. The play ends with the complexity and challenge of holding together commitment to a loving God and the reality of human experience. After finding God guilty, one of the prisoners asks the rabbi who was prosecuting God, "What do we do now?" "Now we pray," was the rabbi's reply.

Wiesel witnessed this event as a child in Auschwitz, when after finding God guilty and a time of stunned silence, the rabbi speaks: "It's time for our evening prayers."[2] It's similar to the experience of Pedro in Wiesel's earlier

1. Dostoevsky, *The Brothers Karamazov*, Book 5, Ch,4, 287
2. Wiesel, *The Trial of God*

novel, *The Town Beyond the Wall*, who learns of the torture of his friend Michael in prison and wants to shout at God in fury at all Michael has gone through, but "the shout becomes a prayer in spite of me."

Cottrell-Boyce, writing in *The Guardian* in 2008 about his drama ending with the call to pray, saw it not as stoicism, nor a failure of courage. It was the refusal of human beings to become dehumanized components in a Nazi project, even if their bodies ended up as that. It was faith, because in the end, said Cottrell-Boyce, "the human is irreducible."[3]

2. Have suffering and death always been part of the evolutionary process?

Suffering and physical death have existed throughout the history of our universe. The life and death of stars provided the elements for all carbon-based life that exists in our world. The fossil record begins more than three and a half billion years ago. From early microscopic life forms and all through the development of cellular life forms, birth and death have been the experience of all biological organisms.

We can easily forget that God's gift of freedom for humanity to make choices and take responsibility can only make sense if the same gift of freedom is also given to the world we live in. This means freedom for the universe in its evolutionary process. John Polkinghorne calls it "love's gift of freedom," with freedom for the processes of the cosmos as the essential partner to freedom for human beings.[4] There are two limitations on that freedom. One is what we observe as natural laws governing all that happens, and the second is divine intervention to ensure God's ultimate purposes are fulfilled.

Predation, violence, conflict and suffering were part of life on earth during the billions of years before the emergence of homo sapiens, and five early mass extinctions have shaped the history of the earth.[5] The evolutionary process has been full of pain and suffering and ending in death, but it has also been complex, diverse, efficient, and progressively transformative. The five mass extinctions that changed life on earth put a stop to many possibilities, but also allowed changes of direction. As homo sapiens, we are

3. Cottrell-Boyce, *Losing My Religion*

4. Polkinghorne, *Science and Providence*, 75–77

5. Ordovician c.450 million years ago, Devonian c.375 mya, Permian c.250 mya, Triassic c.200 mya, Cretaceous c.66 mya.

beneficiaries of the extinction of dinosaurs around sixty-six million years ago. Their disappearance opened the way for the age of mammals to replace the age of reptiles.[6] Humanity, of course, has greatly increased suffering with our selfish, destructive behaviour, and we must take responsibility for much of the terrible and unnecessary pain that humans and other creatures suffer.

3. Can we believe in a God who loves us when the world is full of suffering?

Paul wrote his letter called Romans before he had been to the city where he ended up being executed, but he knew enough about Rome from his friends there. He knew it could be a brutal place, ruled over by cruel emperors in Paul's time, like Tiberius, Caligula, Claudius, and Nero.

When he wrote to the Christians in Rome, Paul assured them that the one thing that is greater than all the suffering people have to face is the love of God, shown in the life, death and resurrection of Jesus Christ. "Who will separate us from the love of Christ? Will tribulation, or distress, or persecution, or famine, or nakedness, or peril, or sword?"[7] These were examples of suffering all too familiar to people living in Rome,[8] but Paul is sure that "neither death, nor life, nor angels, nor principalities, nor things present, nor things to come, nor powers, nor height, nor depth, nor any other created thing, will be able to separate us from the love of God, which is in Christ Jesus our Lord."[9]

Knowing there is no force in the universe greater than the love of God allows Paul to remind the Roman Christians that "what we are suffering now is nothing compared with our future glory" in God's new earth.[10] Paul's claim that our future condition will transform our perception of life's suffering helps to explain why God has taken the risk of giving both us and the universe itself the gift of freedom.

6. UCL, *Mammal diversity*
7. Rom 8:35
8. Burnett, *Paul Distilled*, ch.1
9. Rom 8:38–39
10. Rom 8:18

45

4. Can we find any solutions to the problem of suffering?

In answer to question 5 in chapter 2, "Modern Science and Christian Faith," we looked at two different starting points for thinking about the presence of suffering in the world during the millions of years before humans arrived on the scene. The search for a satisfying theodicy (a defence of God's goodness, love, power and wisdom in the face of the realities of suffering and evil in the world) that includes human history has been a constant challenge. I suggest four aspects of a theodicy here, with emphasis on the need for all four to be held together.

I can understand N. T. Wright's warning that we can be so absorbed with finding theoretical answers to questions, such as the existence of supernatural evil, that we fail to put our attention on what he calls a practical theodicy, the task given to all who follow Jesus to build his kingdom and help clear up the mess that evil creates.

(i) The soul-making explanation

John Hick's 1966 book, *Evil and the God of Love*, became instantly celebrated for what Hick called the "soul-making" role of suffering in human life. Hick's view was that we need to pass through a "vale of soul-making" to help develop us as truly moral beings. Suffering has been an integral part of our universe's evolving process, and while the soul-making view doesn't see God as a cause of suffering, it is a way God uses for us to learn love and care, sympathy and compassion, strength and persistence, wisdom and self-realization.

Richard Rohr sees God turning suffering into a tool for human transformation,[11] allowing us some understanding of the place of hardship and endurance in human life. Only a universe with freedom makes human development possible. A perfect world would be static and not a place for human development. Suffering is an integral part of that process. Christopher Southgate, in his book *The Groaning of Creation*, sums up one role of suffering in preparing us for God's new creation in the world to come. We need to experience the world as it is because "heaven can eternally preserve the selves God wishes us to become, but it could not give rise to them in the first place."[12] This means allowing freedom for the world to evolve in

11. Rohr, *The Universal Christ*, 207
12. Southgate, *The Groaning of Creation*, 90

the way that it has, and not, as Austin Farrar writes, removing "the physical realm of its physicality."[13]

The soul-making explanation takes us one step along the way to understanding a role for suffering, but it doesn't explain the depths that suffering can reach in the lives of many people, and especially in the worst of history's atrocities.

(ii) Our human responsibility

It's obvious that we greatly increase the amount of suffering in the world by our own self-centred, destructive behaviour. We must take responsibility for a huge amount of the terrible and unnecessary pain suffered by people and the whole animal kingdom.

Traditionally, a distinction has been made between moral evil (evil actions for which human beings must take responsibility) and natural evil (natural disasters in which human responsibility isn't directly involved). However, it's clear, and becoming clearer all the time, that the way we treat our natural environment plays a significant part in contributing to natural disasters.

(iii) God on the cross

The third step is that Jesus shared the worst of human experience, and God has transformed human suffering on the cross into a means of victory over evil. God is the crucified one, our fellow sufferer who fully understands what it is to be human. God's presence with us means no suffering is experienced alone, while the creation itself waits in eager expectation for the new earth to be established.[14]

As John Stott explained in his book, *The Cross of Christ*, God's masterstroke in showing the depth of his love and his commitment to us is by following us into the realities of human life and experiencing the worst that we can do to each other. Paul explains how our experience of a God "who comforts us in all our troubles" becomes a gift "so that we can comfort those in any trouble with the comfort we ourselves have received from God."[15]

13. Farrar, *Love Almighty*, 51

14. Rom 8:19

15. 2 Cor 1:4

God's support for us doesn't explain why we suffer, but it assures us that no suffering is experienced without God's intimate sharing of his presence.

(iv) All able to say that the glory to come will eclipse the evil and the suffering

This is the aspect that's often missing from theodicies. I'm grateful for the thoughts of two remarkable theologians, Keith Ward in *The Big Questions in Science and Religion,* and Christopher Southgate in *The Groaning of Creation: God, Evolution, and the Problem of Evil.*

Ward is clear that if we believe in the biblical assurance of a recreated, renewed universe, then it must include "the outweighing of evil with good" for all who have suffered, for "one person's suffering cannot morally be outweighed by another person's flourishing."[16] Christopher Southgate is equally clear. Once all things have been reconciled and unified in Christ, every living creature must be able to say that the joy of the destination exceeded all the pains of the journey. This is because a loving God cannot regard any of his creatures as "a mere evolutionary expedient."[17]

Southgate uses the word "creature" rather than "person," because he wants to emphasize that it's the whole creation that is the focus of God's loving care, in line with John's vision in Revelation when he sees and hears every living creature worshipping God,[18] for this is the ultimate meaning of Christ's victory on the cross.

When Peter spoke to the crowds after the day of Pentecost, he explained that Jesus, who had risen from the dead and ascended to heaven, "must remain in heaven until the time of universal restoration that God announced long ago through his holy prophets."[19] The repeated promise in both the Old and New Testaments is "a new heaven and a new earth" in the future, when the whole created universe will be renewed and restored. There are no limits to God's plan to renew and restore, for God's salvation is cosmic and universal.

Some will complain that this sounds like a form of compensation in the world to come for the extremities of pain, grief and suffering here and now. I don't accept that. I've called this section "all able to say that the glory

16. Ward, *The Big Questions in Science and Religion,* 51

17. Southgate, *The Groaning of Creation,* 16

18. Rev 5:13

19. Acts 3:21 (NRSVue)

to come will eclipse the evil and the suffering," because when you put together Hick's soul-making explanation, Southgate's view that the heaven to come requires earthly experience to prepare us, and Paul's view that "our present sufferings are not worth comparing with the glory that will be revealed in us,"[20] the horrors of the worst of present suffering are certainly not underestimated, but neither is the reality of the glory in the world to come.

This has to be held alongside our proper desire for justice in the world to come. We see a consistent theme in the Bible of God's judgment, but it's a judgment that is never simply punitive, but always productive with a positive purpose and outcome. As John Oswalt writes in his commentary on the book of Isaiah, "judgment is never God's last word, but his intention is to use judgment to bring about lasting hope."[21] I'm aware that all of this raises many questions, and I try to deal with these in detail and provide biblical responses in chapter 6, "The New Creation: Universal Restoration."

5. What about the suffering of non-human animals?

The Natural Resources Defense Council has much to say about "the crucial role that predators play in protecting and sustaining their surrounding environments and ecosystems."[22] We can accept that predation has an important role to play in the evolutionary process, but it's still a huge moral problem for anyone who sees our universe as the creation of a loving God. John Stuart Mill sums up his objection satirically in his essay "On Nature." "If there are any marks of special design in creation, one of the things most evidently designed is that a large proportion of all animals should pass their existence in tormenting and devouring other animals."[23]

Colin Gunton, in his investigation of the purpose of Christ's incarnation, emphasizes that God's concern with humans is always in the context of the whole creation, and this will also apply to God's new creation.[24] Theologian Ernst Conradie argues effectively that any answer to the moral problem of suffering must be seen in the context of the death of Jesus, not only to redeem humanity, but to redeem the whole cosmos. He suggests

20. Rom 8:18

21. Oswalt, *The NIV Application Commentary: Isaiah*, 43

22. Natural Resources Defense Council, *The Ecological Importance of Predators*

23. Mill, *Nature*

24. Gunton, *Christ and Creation*, 33–34

that through the redemptive work of Christ, nothing will be lost in the ultimate transformation. Christ's redemptive work will result in "an embodied celebration" from which no living creature will be excluded.[25]

Only the total inclusiveness in the "embodied celebration" that will come with God's new creation can address the negative aspects of the evolutionary process, not just on human and animal life in general, but on the individual sparrow, not one of whom "can fall to the ground without your Father knowing it."[26] "If we were to surrender hope for as much as one single creature, God would not be God," writes Jurgen Moltmann.[27]

I leave the last word on this subject to John Wesley, in his 1781 sermon called "The General Deliverance." Speaking of the wonderful variety of God's creation, Wesley insisted that for all God's creatures "something better remains after death, that these likewise shall one day be delivered from this bondage of corruption, and shall then receive an ample amends for all their present sufferings."[28]

The question of animal suffering in the evolutionary process before humans arrived on the scene is discussed in more detail in chapter 2, "Modern Science and Christian Faith," question 11, on why evolution has involved waste, destruction and suffering,

6. Can we explain the existence of evil?

If God made the universe and saw that everything was very good,[29] and Paul tells us that "in Christ, all things were created: things in heaven and on earth, visible and invisible, whether thrones or powers or rulers or authorities; all things have been created through him and for him,"[30] then how could evil appear in the good creation?

We can speculate that because "God is love,"[31] and love needs to be freely given, that need for free choice may also be the case with created spiritual beings beyond our material universe. But there may be a reason why we don't know how evil originated. French theologian, Henri Blocher,

25. Conradie, *Resurrection, Finitude and Ecology*

26. Matt 10:9

27. Moltmann, *The Coming of God*, 132

28. Wesley, *The General Deliverance*, 523–31

29. Gen 1:31

30. Col 1:16

31. 1 John 4:8

in his book *Evil and the Cross: An Analytical Look at the Problem of Pain*, makes an important point about the origin of evil. After surveying the question of evil from every point of view, Blocher unapologetically claims that perhaps evil must remain a mystery.

To explain it would enable us to understand it, and to understand it would go some way to rationalize, justify and even excuse it. It must and does remain ultimately indescribable and inexcusable. Neil Messer, writing about evolution and theodicy, makes the same point. "By attempting to explain it, we risk rationalizing it, and giving it a place in the world to which it is not entitled."[32]

I'm reminded of the books of Auschwitz survivor and Nobel laureate, Elie Wiesel, about the Holocaust. As Michael Berenbaum writes, Wiesel "offered entry into a new way of speaking," because it was "essential to his worldview that the Holocaust was truly incomprehensible and inexplicable."[33]

God's gift of freedom both to humanity and to the evolving universe contains within itself the possibility of producing people and actions that we can call evil. C. S. Lewis, in his book *Mere Christianity*, writes about freedom to choose as an essential part of God's goal to create a world in which love and goodness are more than the responses of mechanical automata.[34]

Evil also has religious connotations of dark forces behind the scenes working against all that is good. When Paul writes that "our struggle is not against flesh and blood, but against the rulers, against the authorities, against the powers of this dark world and against the spiritual forces of evil in the heavenly realms,"[35] we see his conviction about their reality, but what sort of entities they are remains mysterious.

N. T. Wright points out the difficulty for us as modern people to cope with what seemed common in earlier ages, that there were all kinds of "complex hierarchies" in the universe: nine orders of angels and all kinds of rebellious devils and demons. We may quite rightly feel that we need to leave that medieval worldview behind, but at the same time, we can take seriously Shakespeare's words spoken by Hamlet, that "there are more things in heaven and earth, Horatio, than are dreamt of in your philosophy."

---

32. Messer, "Evolution and Theodicy."

33. Berenbaum, *Elie Wiesel*

34. Lewis, *Mere Christianity*, 48

35. Eph 6:12

A crucial aspect of the reality of evil is the attempts of dark powers to influence and if possible, to take over our personal, social and political lives and structures. Walter Wink helps us by identifying some of these influences in the world that can have evil outcomes: impersonal, dominating forces that enslave human beings caught in power structures such as materialism, consumerism, capitalism, communism, militarism, nationalism, imperialism and racism, (that lead to examples such as slavery, Ku Klux Klan, ISIS, Naziism and Auschwitz).[36] What is clear is that God's salvation is cosmic in scale, and spiritual warfare is the kingdom of God battling the powers that enslave and destroy, in order to liberate all caught in their power structures.

What we know about the "powers and principalities," both human and spiritual ones, as Paul describes them, is that when Jesus had "disarmed the powers and authorities, he made a public spectacle of them, triumphing over them by the cross." But that is not the end. The future is God's intention through Jesus, "to reconcile to himself all things, whether things on earth or things in heaven, by making peace through his blood, shed on the cross."[37]

Only our belief in a God of love and wisdom allows us to say that reconciliation will be God's promised ultimate outcome. Julian of Norwich's profound claim that "all shall be well and all manner of thing shall be well"[38] takes seriously the restoration and renewal of all things, enabled by the victory of Jesus on the cross.

What distinguishes evil from goodness and love is that evil is not an ultimate reality. The only ultimate reality is the community of love we call the Trinity, three divine persons whose perfection of love makes them one God. Unlike love, the existence of evil is temporary and will one day cease to exist. We are assured that evil and all its forms will one day be completely ended in the new creation, which is the ultimate and guaranteed goal of God's whole creative purpose. This is the truly good news of the Christian gospel. The ending of Timothy Rees's beautiful hymn, written just after the ending of the First World War, "God is Love, let heaven adore him" sums up the truth that the post-war world needed to know: "God is Love, so Love for ever o'er the universe must reign."[39] Rob Bell develops the same emphasis in his recent book, *Love Wins: At the Heart of Life's Big Questions*, where he

36. Wink, *The Powers That Be*
37. Col 2:15 & 1:20
38. Julian of Norwich, *Revelations of Divine Love*, ch.27
39. Community of the Resurrection, *Mirfield Mission*

shows how the biblical message of God's love and grace is the ultimate truth and beauty of the Christian good news.

7. Why does God allow disasters?

The Covid19 global pandemic gives us a clue as to why God's creation is the way it is. We wouldn't have life on earth without viruses. Most scientists agree that viruses enabled cellular life to begin around four billion years ago, and viruses still contribute to human life in various ways. But they can also mutate into vicious killers. Immunotherapy uses specially engineered viruses to treat cancer, but we also have ancient viruses buried in our DNA that can reawaken and attack us again. Why would God allow the universe freedom to evolve, causing destruction as well as promoting what is good and beautiful?

It's not helpful to simplify and just call disasters "acts of God". Human injustice, greed, inequality and neglect, with resulting poverty and vulnerability, make their own contribution to disasters. Our present threat of climate change is an obvious example, making disasters more frequent, with the most vulnerable most badly affected.

I've already referred to Bill Vanstone's claim that God treats both humanity and the cosmos with respect, giving to each the "gift of love" which is freedom, knowing that freedom also means vulnerability.[40] John Polkinghorne comes to the same conclusion. In relation to both moral evil (the results of human sin) and natural evil (disasters in nature), God is "not the puppet master of men or matter."[41] Polkinghorne & Beale sum this up well when they explain that the evolutionary process requires chance and necessity to work together. Chance allows the openness for the new to appear, while necessity provides the regularity for the new to be established.[42]

The God whom we meet in Jesus is one whose loving purpose is for the whole of creation to share in the fullness of the divine life and love of the Trinity in a new earth when Jesus returns. Without freedom for our universe to evolve, growth in understanding and love, as well as growth in a whole range of other human values, just couldn't happen, and growth is the only way if one day we are to share in the fullness of divine life.

40. Vanstone, *Love's Endeavour*, 62–63
41. Polkinghorne, *Science and Providence*, 78
42. Polkinghorne, *Questions of Truth*, 142–43

But there's an obvious problem with that. What about those who experience the worst of the suffering? Are they simply sacrificial victims along the way? Is the price paid for God's "gift of love" too great? Keith Ward helps us here. In the end, good must "overwhelmingly outweigh any evils in the cosmic process."[43] Every created being must ultimately be able to say that the experience of the destination outweighed the horrors of the journey.

If an evolving universe with genuine freedom for the whole cosmos inevitably means times of suffering and struggle, then my own conclusion is that if there had been another, less painful way for God to achieve his purpose, God would have used it. The story of science and its discoveries point to the wisdom, love and goodness of God interacting with the freedom given to human beings and to the whole cosmos, so that in the end God's good purposes are achieved.

8. Do miracles happen, and if so, why not more often?

Talk about miracles usually begins with a long discussion about how to define the word miracle. Let me avoid that by suggesting two main types of miracle. One type of miracle is a purposeful event for which, given our present knowledge, we can't find a natural, scientific explanation, and we attribute it to a divine, supernatural cause. The second is where God acts without suspending what we know as natural, scientific laws, but intervenes in our lives through what John Polkinghorne, in *Science and Providence*, calls "arranged coincidence," or providential timing.[44]

Alongside those miraculous interventions are the "ordinary" experiences of a God who is with us all the time in the person of the Holy Spirit, journeying through life with us, helping, guiding, enabling, reminding, challenging, teaching, warning, comforting, strengthening, renewing, energizing, and all the Spirit's other contributions to our everyday lives. There is one source of all that is good, all that is loving, all that is helpful and wise, so it's perfectly sensible to be thanking God, as the source for everything that is good in our lives. Who knows how often God intervenes in our lives without making a great announcement about it?

Acts 2:22 combines three Greek words that relate to God's miraculous work. "Jesus of Nazareth was a man accredited by God to you by acts of power (dunamis), wonders (teras) and signs (semeion), which God did

43. Ward, *The Big Questions*, 51

44. Polkinghorne, *Science and Providence*, 57

among you through him." All three aspects are true of miracles. They are wonders, acts of power and significant signs.

Belief in God obviously means God has no boundaries in relation to what is possible, but if so, why not perform interventions that everyone recognizes as miraculous far more often? One issue is summed up by John Polkinghorne. God acts in many ways that demonstrate his love and compassion, but they don't become "the acts of a capricious, interventionist God."[45]

Part of God's controlling influence is what we call the laws of nature. The laws of nature do not cause things to happen. They simply state the patterns that we experience and thus how we understand our universe, and our knowledge of the laws of nature is limited by our present understanding. One has only to mention quantum theory to see how much we still have to learn.

We wouldn't live in the real world of natural law if God intervened to put things right whenever something went wrong. God would just be a magic-worker and human life as we know it would be meaningless. The regularities of nature demonstrate a consistent, trustworthy God, and make the work of science possible. God's consistency is part of the provision of a loving God to enable us, through the vast range of human experiences, pleasant and unpleasant, to grow into people who can follow the way of Jesus in our lives, and one day share in the fullness of the divine life of the Trinity in the new earth.

Polkinghorne suggests that much of our experience of God's providential working in our lives takes the form of what he calls "arranged coincidences," as a more common form of miracle than God's overriding his own natural laws. My wife and I shared personal examples of two life-transforming events in Pamela's first book, *From Shore to Shore: Living in God's Global Kingdom*, that we regard as this kind of miracle.[46] That still leaves open the question of all the tragedies throughout the world that could be avoided if God just intervened in their timing, and probably all of us can point to events where we were victims of bad timing. As we saw with the general issue of suffering, we trust whole-heartedly in a God whose love for every part of the creation is never-ending.

We know that if God was always to intervene, he'd be a puppeteer manipulating all of human life. One alternative would be never to intervene,

---

45. Polkinghorne, *Science and Providence*, 53–68

46. Ferguson, *From Shore to Shore*, 32–35 & 45–47

but that's certainly not the God we meet in the Bible and who is revealed to us in Jesus Christ. Our human situation means trust in the love and wisdom of God in all that God does. That's an easy sentence to write, but desperately hard to hold on to when our suffering seems beyond what we can bear. Around half of the Psalms are laments, and "How long O Lord? Will you forget me for ever? How long will you hide your face from me?" is a cry the Bible faces up to frequently.

We might ask why God allows the followers of Jesus to suffer terrible persecution and martyrdom. You'd expect that they'd have protection if they're spreading the truth about a God who loves us all. We know that three of Jesus's early followers, Peter, Paul and James, were martyred for their faith, and tradition suggests many of the other disciples suffered torture and death as they travelled to spread the news of Jesus's resurrection. We read in John's gospel about how Jesus spoke to Peter about Peter's future martyrdom.[47] The suffering of Christians in many parts of the world today is well documented. The Bishop of Truro's 2019 *Independent Review of Persecution Worldwide*, found "persecution on grounds of religious faith is a global phenomenon that is growing in scale and intensity . . . with Christians being the most persecuted group."

We really only have two options to choose from. Either the world is a "cosmic lottery" without hope of remediation, as Rachel Held Evans called it in her search for faith,[48] or the big story is true that there is a God who made us, loves us, is with us in all circumstances, and will bring all things ultimately to share in a glorious, restored earth.

Jesus consistently rejected miracles as a way of promoting belief. He refused demands for a sign, and very seldom appealed to his actions as proof of his divinity. It makes good sense for us to ask a loving God to intervene by changing our most challenging circumstances, but the answer often seems to be "my grace is sufficient for you, for my power is made perfect in weakness."[49]

That doesn't mean we should ever stop asking for God's intervention in every situation. The church's ministry of healing has seen miraculous outcomes throughout the world, and we should always ask, sharing Jesus's prayer, "your will be done." What we know is that our prayers are always

---

47. John 21:18–19

48. Evans, *Faith Unraveled*, 148–49

49. 2 Cor 12:8

answered, sometimes with physical outcomes, but always with a deep awareness of God's loving presence and help in all we go through.

We can place the events of our lives in the hands of a God who loves us and shares our pains and is always there to be our help and strength, and who has made himself known in the life, death and resurrection of Jesus. If God wants to use our lives as a window through which other people can get a glimpse of what God is like, then even our vulnerability and weakness can be a way for God to reveal himself. Pamela Ferguson's poem "Window" was written as a tribute to her late father, whose life in so many ways allowed her to see aspects of who God is:

> You are the canvas
> on which the colours of the landscape
> first found shape.
> You are the frame
> that lets the picture speak.
> You built the window
> that lets the spectrum of the sunlight in,
> and when lights go out
> and night comes in
> I see the colours of the stars.[50]

9. Where can we find unshakable hope for the world?

"Pie in the sky when you die" has been the complaint of social activists ever since Joe Hill coined the words in his 1911 song, popularized later by artists like Woody Guthrie and Pete Seeger:

> "You will eat bye and bye
> In that glorious land above the sky.
> Work and pray, live on hay,
> You'll get pie in the sky when you die."[51]

The complaint arises again and again during times of protest. It isn't so much to do with giving people false hope for the future. Its main attack is on religion that is more interested in getting into heaven than in addressing inequality, changing the power structures, providing for the poor and the hungry here and now. We need to show that we're not waiting for the

50. Ferguson, *From Shore to Shore*, 76
51. Industrial Workers, *Little Red Songbook*

future for renewal. Paul tells us that "if anyone is in Christ, he or she is a new creation," and the purpose is to spread that newness into every aspect of our present life.[52]

For a world bereft of hope through warfare, through natural disasters, through mental health problems, through people living with daily problems of all kinds, the Greek word for hope in the Bible is a strong word. The verb "elpo" means to "confidently expect" and that is the hope Jesus brings. The Jesus we meet in the gospels is focused on bringing hope to people in their present circumstances. The focus of God's new creation is on the world as it is now, for God's kingdom has come and God's calling to us is to spread it throughout the whole world.

It's a task in progress, to be completed when Jesus returns to finish the "universal restoration" that Peter talked about in his second speech to the crowds after the Day of Pentecost.[53] There's a special merit in the translation of the "apokatastasis" in Acts 3:21 as "universal restoration,"[54] for the whole universe is the focus of God's renewal, and Peter in his speech links the apokatastasis with the promise to Abraham that "all peoples on the earth will be blessed."[55]

God's new creation is here and now as we seek for his "will to be done on earth, as it is in heaven,"[56] but there's also the hope Paul refers to when he's in prison in Rome and doesn't have long to live. He writes to his fellow-worker Titus about "the hope for life in the age to come, which God, who does not lie, promised before the beginning of time."[57] The big story of the Bible is God with us in all life's challenges and into God's new creation in the age to come, our "living hope through the resurrection of Jesus Christ."[58] Our message in word and action needs to show, as Thomas Talbott claims, that "the truth about the universe is ultimately glorious, not tragic."[59]

52. 2 Cor 5:17

53. Acts 3:21

54. NRSVue

55. Acts 3: 25

56. Matt 6:10

57. Titus 1:2

58. 1 Pet 1:3

59. Parry, *Universal Salvation?* 265

Further Discussion

1. Do you agree that suffering was part of life on earth long before humans appeared?

2. Why is life so unfair, with suffering much more extreme for some people than for others?

3. If you had been in the group of prisoners in Auschwitz debating whether or not to find God guilty for what they were suffering, how might you have voted?

4. What do you think about the claim that in the world to come, all will be able to say that the glory far outweighs the sufferings of the journey?

5. Do you agree with Jonathan Southgate that belief in a God who loves us means no creature can be just collateral damage in the evolutionary process?

Chapter 5

The Trinity & the Cross of Christ

1. What does it mean to call God a Trinity?
2. What's the meaning of the cross of Christ?

- love

- our predicament

- sacrifice

- rescue

- resurrection

1. What does it mean to call God a Trinity?

The Shema, the Jewish morning and evening prayer, starts with the most fundamental belief in Judaism: monotheism. "Hear, O Israel: the Lord our God, the Lord is one," or sometimes translated "Hear, O Israel: The Lord is our God, the Lord alone." In Islam, Allah is Al Ahad, the Only One, the Unique, the One who has ever been and ever remains alone. Belief in the oneness and unity of Allah is the first of the Five Pillars of Islam. For Muslims, the Christian claim that God is a Trinity sounds like blasphemy.

The fact is that Christianity is also monotheistic in its belief in the oneness and unity of God. The wonderful theme that runs through both the Old and New Testaments is that God is one, not in the sense of isolated solitude, but in relationship, in community, a Trinity of three whose life and love are indivisible. Love is a unifying emotion. It shouldn't be difficult to

60

see that a divine perfection of infinite love means that three are fully and indivisibly one.

Jewish and Muslim people put great emphasis on the transcendent perfection of Yahweh or Allah. The Muslim concept of transcendent perfection doesn't recognize that relationship must be part of oneness for love to be perfect. In his commentary on John's Gospel, Roy Millar writes that "allusions to relationship within the Godhead" were already recognized by some Jewish scholars before the time of Jesus.[1] He points to Old Testament allusions in Genesis 1:26, Proverbs 30:4, Isaiah 48:16 and Psalm 110:1. Perfection of love in the Godhead encompasses relationship and community, just as love in community is the expression of our humanity, created in God's image.

When John writes in his first letter that "God is love,"[2] he tells us that love is the very essence of the being of God. As Len Vander Zee points out, it's difficult to understand the meaning of love in complete singleness of being. The God we worship is an eternal community of love at the centre of reality, so that our universe becomes "an overflow of love from that original divine community."[3] Our greatest calling is to experience that love, and reflect it in all our human relationships.

The apostle John is clear in his view of the Christology of Jesus (the person and role of Jesus as the Messiah), and the oneness in plurality of Father, Son and Holy Spirit. Jesus is the Word who was God and with God in the beginning.[4] Jesus, as the Word made flesh, is clear about both his person and his role. "I and the Father are one,"[5] and "anyone who has seen me has seen the Father."[6] Incorporated into that oneness is the Spirit of God. "I will ask the Father, and he will give you another Counsellor to be with you for ever, the Spirit of truth."[7]

It's clear that the threefold unity of the Trinity was the basis of the early church's belief and worship. Early in Matthew's gospel we have the baptism of Jesus in which Father, Son, and Holy Spirit are present and active.[8] The

---

1. Millar, *Come and See* 31
2. 1 John 4:8
3. Zee, *The Holy Trinity*
4. John 1:1–2
5. John 10:30
6. John 14:9
7. John 14: 16–17
8. Matt 3: 16–17

gospel ends with the call for the disciples to "go and make disciples of all nations, baptizing them in the name of the Father and of the Son and of the Holy Spirit."[9] The apostles Peter and Paul use the same language of Father, Son and Holy Spirit.[10]

We only have human attempts to give names to the threefold essence of God, calling God Father, Son and Holy Spirit. Speaking of God in human, family terms may be the nearest we can get to describing the divine, but it shouldn't give the impression that the Father existed before the Son or the Spirit. God is eternal and uncreated, existing in threefold community.

The other issue is the masculine language used in the Bible and throughout the history of the Christian church. Shirley Isaac, in her article "God-Language and Gender: Some Trinitarian Reflections" argues convincingly that inclusive and female language is not only "compatible with God's self-revelation," but may well provide a corrective emphasis to some assumptions about God. At the same time, she recognizes that it could raise "more difficulties than it resolves" to change the present trinitarian baptismal language in many contemporary cultures.[11]

Darrell Johnson, in *Experiencing the Trinity*, sums up the truth about the Trinity of love. God who is Father, Son, and Holy Spirit, "draws near to us and draws us into and within the circle of his being, into the inner fellowship of the community."[12] The website "Music and Dancing" has collected some of the most beautiful expressions of the dance of love that is the life of the Trinity.[13] It's only when we grasp something of the beauty of God as Trinity that we can truly see the Trinity as the home we want to live in now and in the life to come.

Glendalough in the Wicklow mountains on the east coast of Ireland is famous as an early Christian monastic settlement founded by St. Kevin in the 6th century. A major part of the focus of nearby Glendalough Hermitage Centre is sharing Celtic Christianity,[14] and the Centre website includes a focus on the Trinity as central to Celtic spirituality, that experienced the presence of God as Trinity in the natural world, and in every aspect of daily life. The prayers of St Patrick are filled with images of the encircling

---

9. Matt 28: 19

10. 1 Pet 1:2 and 2 Cor 13:14

11. Isaac, "God-Language and Gender"

12. Johnson, *Experiencing the Trinity*, ch.3

13. Music and Dancing, "The dance of love"

14. Glendalough Hermitage Centre, "Spirituality"

presence of the Trinity, with St Patrick's Breastplate probably the best known. In 1889, Irish poet, Cecil Frances Alexander, published a beautiful metrical version of the eighth century Old Gaelic hymn, traditionally ascribed to St Patrick, that ends:

> I bind unto myself the Name,
> The strong Name of the Trinity;
> By invocation of the same,
> The Three in One, and One in Three,
> Of Whom all nature hath creation;
> Eternal Father, Spirit, Word:
> Praise to the Lord of my salvation,
> Salvation is of Christ the Lord. [15]

2. What is the meaning of the cross of Christ?

N. T. Wright's book, *The Day the Revolution Began: Rethinking the Meaning of Jesus's Crucifixion*, provides a detailed discussion of what he calls the place where "all narratives of human history converge." Parts of this discussion are followed up in many helpful short videos on YouTube summarizing his views, such as "Atonement Theology" and "The Cross."

(i) Love

The meaning of the Trinity is that God is a community of love living in perfect oneness. The incarnation, when God entered our world as a fully human being, means Jesus was the embodiment of the Triune God who was identifying fully and completely with our human existence and human experience.

Whatever else we say about the crucifixion of Jesus, the love of God for humanity and the whole created world will always be the central reality. "God so loved the world that he gave his only Son," writes John in his gospel.[16] John's first letter tells us: "This is how we know what love is: Jesus Christ laid down his life for us."[17] If we talk about the anger of God being shown in the cross of Christ, Paul makes it clear that the objects of God's

---

15. Wright, *The Writings of St. Patrick*
16. John 3:16
17. 1 John 3:16

anger are the sin and evil that have caused so much suffering in the world. Christ is our "sin offering, and so God condemned sin in sinful man."[18] It was incomparable love that allowed Jesus to completely identify himself with the penalty that we brought upon ourselves by our turning away from all that God wants for created life.

(ii) Our predicament

Our biggest problem is humanity's tendency to make little gods of things like wealth, power, success, status, our own selves or our own family, and the result is the world we live in, a world of inequality, pain and grief. God's world was never meant to be like that.

In the Bible, the Greek word "hamartia" was commonly used for our failure as individuals and as societies to reflect the love, goodness and harmony of God. It means missing the mark, not fulfilling the intended purpose. The two great commandments that Jesus taught us show how very far we are from the life God wants for us. "Love the Lord your God with all your heart and with all your soul and with all your mind," and "love your neighbour as yourself."[19] It's not hard to see that life today for humanity, for the animal world, and for the environment, isn't the place of care and love that God intended. Of course, there are wonderful examples of selfless service and self-sacrifice for the sake of others, but the big picture is that human nature misses the mark, the ideal that God intended.

Our choice to live life in separation from God has resulted in the loss of so much potential for humankind and for the world. Jesus came to show us how to live a human life, and a significant part of that was communicating with God, recognizing that God is the source of all wisdom and goodness. Our separation from God has meant that the last word about life for every one of us is death.

(iii) Sacrifice

Built into every legal system is the idea that giving up something precious to yourself (like money, or time, or freedom) is needed to pay for wrongdoing. Without that, there's little opportunity for justice, and the hope is that

18. Rom 8:3–4
19. Matt 22:37–39

the loss of something precious will be a learning experience that wrongdoing needs to be avoided if life is to function properly.

In Jesus's Jewish practice, in a country where wealth was usually held in livestock, sacrifices of animals were carried out every day as a way of paying for the sins of the people. When John the Baptist met Jesus, he called him "the Lamb of God who takes away the sins of the world."[20] He understood the prophecies about Jesus, that he would be God's way of paying for the sins of the whole world, once and for all, never needing to be repeated, with a sacrifice of his own life.

The writer of the book of Hebrews described the Jewish sacrificial system as a shadow pointing to the reality that the Messiah would achieve. The sacrificial system just reminded people of guilt, without doing anything to improve their lives. The book of Hebrews quotes Psalm 40 as a prophecy about Jesus, whose death on the cross would open the way to free us from sin and guilt. "Sacrifice and offering you did not desire, but a body you prepared for me. With burnt offerings and sin offerings you were not pleased. Then I said, 'Here I am—it is written about me in the scroll—I have come to do your will, my God.'"[21]

(iv) Rescue

For God, the creator of all life, to come into the world himself and suffer the ultimate punishment, despite having done nothing but good, is what makes Christianity completely unique among all religions. God's answer to our condition meant coming and living our life in the person of Jesus, demonstrating how the love and goodness of God could be reflected in a life lived in close relationship with God and in service of others.

Paul's message in his letter to the Romans was that laws and moral codes were never going to be enough to change human nature. By sending Jesus to show what human nature was always meant to be, God condemned the sin and evil that infected human nature.[22] Even on the cross, Jesus was still working to restore our relationship with God, praying "Father, forgive them, for they do not know what they are doing."[23]

20. John 1:29
21. Ps 40:5–7
22. Rom 8:3–4
23. Luke 23:34

Jesus identified with us in all the challenges of life, including our suffering and death. In experiencing the worst that we can do to each other, in his humiliation and crucifixion, he took upon himself the forces of evil that have such a dominating impact on us and our world. As Paul describes it, God "reconciled to himself all things, by making peace through his blood shed on the cross," so that "there is now no condemnation for those who are in Christ Jesus," for Jesus "has set you free from the law of sin and death."[24]

Charles Wesley's great 1762 hymn captures that recurring moment of realization that it is the eternal God in the person of Jesus who has died to achieve our forgiveness: "'Tis finished! The Messiah dies, / cut off for sin, but not his own; / accomplished is the sacrifice, / the great redeeming work is done," for "the grand and full atonement made; / God for a guilty world hath died."[25]

(v) Resurrection

The last enemy for all of us and for all created life is death, and the resurrection of Jesus three days after being buried in the tomb validates everything that Jesus said about his life's purpose. He "has been declared with power to be the Son of God by his resurrection from the dead: Jesus Christ our Lord."[26] Describing how Jesus has defeated the power of evil, Paul writes that he "disarmed the powers and authorities . . . triumphing over them by the cross."[27]

When Peter spoke to the crowd after the day of Pentecost, he told them that Jesus "must remain in heaven until the time of universal restoration that God announced long ago through his holy prophets."[28] Peter's listeners from a Jewish background knew the Old Testament expectation of a Messianic age when the Jewish Davidic kingdom would be restored, and the great promise to Abraham would be realized, that "all peoples on earth will be blessed.[29]

For Peter, the resurrection of Jesus blew that expectation wide open, because not only have sin and evil been defeated on the cross, but Jesus has

24. Col 1:20 & Rom 8:1–2

25. Huntingdon's, *Select Collection of Hymns*

26. Rom 1:4

27. Col 2:15

28. Acts 3:21 (NRSVue)

29. Acts 3: 25

won victory over death itself, and has told his disciples to "go and make disciples of all nations, baptizing them in the name of the Father and of the Son and of the Holy Spirit, and teaching them to obey everything I have commanded you, and surely I am with you always, to the very end of the age."[30]

God's new creation has begun and will continue until Jesus returns to complete the restoration of all things. As well as being the means of forgiveness and new relationship with God, the self-sacrificial example of the cross has become the guide for how we live our lives, and now, as Paul writes to the Galatian church, "the only thing that counts is faith expressing itself through love."[31]

Further Discussion

1. Does knowing God is a Trinity help us understand "God is love"?

2. Is it a problem to use masculine language to describe the three persons of the Trinity?

3. Is it true to say that the main thing we learn from the cross of Christ is not an angry God but a God of love?

4. Was the cross of Jesus God's answer to the problem of evil?

5. What does it mean to have the cross as a model for our lives?

6. Do you think our failure to keep the two great commandments, loving God with all our being, and loving our neighbor as ourselves, is a good way to explain the word "sin" nowadays?

30. Matt 28:19–20
31. Gal 5:6

Chapter 6

The Evidence for the Resurrection of Jesus

1. Introduction: resurrection, history, and the meaning of evidence

2. What's the historical evidence for the resurrection of Jesus?

- Jesus predicted his death and resurrection on several occasions.

- repeated meetings of many people with the risen Jesus.

- Jesus's burial tomb was empty and no dead body was ever found.

- there was no ongoing burial site for Jesus, despite its importance in Jewish tradition.

- many written accounts of Jesus's resurrection based on eye-witness reports.

- multiple eye-witnesses and other followers suffered and died for their belief in Jesus's resurrection.

- fast growth of Christianity only happened because of Jesus's resurrection.

- early Christian writers saw the resurrection as the event that changed everything.

- non-Christian historians commented on the new religion based on resurrection.

- the lives of billions of people transformed by their encounter with the risen Jesus.

3. What process might our resurrection take?

4. If Jesus was Emmanuel, (God with us), why did he not come earlier?

5. How will our present material world connect to God's future new earth?

1. Introduction: resurrection, history, and the meaning of evidence

For the evidence gathered here, there are many excellent discussions by experts in a variety of fields whose books have given us a wide-ranging analysis of the resurrection accounts. Some of those helpful investigations are:

Norman Anderson. *Christianity: The Witness of History*. Carol Stream, IL, Tyndale, 1969.

F.F. Bruce. *The New Testament Documents: Are They Reliable?* London, IVP, 2000.

Josh McDowell. *The New Evidence that Demands a Verdict*. Nashville, TN, Nelson, 1999.

Frank Morison. *Who Moved the Stone?* Milton Keynes, Authentic Media, 2006.

Graeme Smith. *Was the Tomb Empty?* Oxford, Monarch, 2014.

N.T. Wright. *The Resurrection of the Son of God*. London, SPCK, 2017.

Christianity began with a message that changed the world. Death is not the end of life. After death, God raises us to a new existence. That's why the followers of Jesus travelled all over the Roman empire spreading the news that Jesus had died on a Roman cross, but he rose from the dead and spent time with many people who were eye-witnesses of his resurrection.

Belief that Jesus was not just a very special person, but was part of the Godhead that we call the Trinity, makes the historical evidence for his resurrection all the more essential. The idea that the eternal, divine creator of the universe came to earth and allowed himself to be crucified and buried in a grave is so astonishing that only the most convincing evidence for resurrection can make the whole story believable.

When Paul was arrested and brought before the Roman governor Felix, he was clear about what he was being charged with. "It is because of the resurrection of the dead that I am on trial before you today."[1] Paul's impassioned words expressed one of the central claims that allowed Christianity to grow into a worldwide force for good: "O death, where is your sting? O grave, where is your victory?"[2] Earlier he had explained that "Christ was raised from the dead, never to die again."[3]

The reason we have historians is to try to sort out truth from fiction about the past. Primary sources for the truth of an event are evidence from eye-witnesses or contemporaries, the more of them and the closer of the report to the date the better. In fact, we have a remarkable number of primary sources for the life, death and resurrection of Jesus.

Some people say that many of those primary sources are in the New Testament and therefore they're not reliable, objective sources. That is muddled thinking. It's a misunderstanding of what these primary sources are. A growing number of independently written texts about Christ and Christianity appeared during the centuries after Jesus's life, death and resurrection, and the New Testament was a collection of separate first and second century documents that were considered either eye-witness accounts or accounts validated by eye-witnesses. It wasn't until the end of the 4th century that the church officially collected together those individual documents that came to be known as the New Testament.[4]

You might ask why, if we have such a wonderful amount of primary evidence, we can't open any history book about the Roman empire and find references to Jesus's resurrection. North of Palestine was Syria and south was Egypt, two big countries important to Rome. What went on in Palestine was never going to hit the headlines. Also, an important aspect of the historian's approach will always be to look for a "natural" explanation and there is huge reluctance ever to accept the possibility of a supernatural event or miracle, which is then left to theologians to deal with.

I think we can do better than that. Historians should be bound by the same scientific method as other academic researchers. A worldview that says we only deal with natural events, and we all know that dead people don't rise again, and therefore Jesus didn't rise, is not a scientific approach to history. It's even more irresponsible to decide the answer before the evidence has been properly investigated.

1. Acts 24:21
2. 1 Cor 15:55
3. Rom 6:9
4. Rom 6:9

N. T. Wright, in his classic book, *The Resurrection of the Son of God*, starts with two of the key pieces of evidence: the empty tomb with the fact that no dead body of Jesus was ever discovered, and the meetings hundreds of people claimed to have had with the risen Jesus. Wright explains that these pieces of evidence are open to normal historical investigation, and this is especially important because there's no other way we can account for the remarkable growth of early Christianity.[5]

Wright calls them "provable" events, not in some absolute sense, but according to the degree of certainty that historians normally use to refer to an event in history as reliably true. The reason Wright gives is clear. We cannot explain the words and actions of the early Christians and their impact without the claim that Jesus rose from the dead. In other words, the resurrection is a "necessary" condition, as there is simply no other explanation for what the early Christians said, and what they suffered and died for. Resurrection is the only plausible explanation of the evidence.

There's one other aspect of historical investigation that makes the resurrection different from other events in the past. If we discover that Julius Caesar was assassinated by some of his senators in 44BC, it's an interesting historical fact. If we discover that Jesus was raised from the dead around 33AD, that's what Wright calls "a self-committing statement." It means we're committed to working out the implications for our lives here and now.

"The truth shall set you free,"[6] said Jesus, and the truth of Christianity depends on this unique event that changed the course of human history. As with all historical events and scientific claims, believing it depends on the reliability of the evidence. If the resurrection of Jesus took place, then Jesus and his claims are vitally important for every one of us and can transform our lives. If the resurrection did not happen, then Paul is right to say that the whole Christian faith is futile and based on deception. The great Swiss theologian, Karl Barth, summed up what the resurrection of Jesus means when he wrote, "take away the resurrection, and you have taken away . . . the last hope there is for us on earth."[7]

---

5. Wright, *The Resurrection*, ch.18
6. John 8:32
7. Barth, *Come Holy Spirit*, 299

2. What's the historical evidence for the resurrection of Jesus?

(i) Jesus predicted his own death and resurrection on several occasions

Jesus was aware that he was facing increasing opposition that would lead to his death and all four gospels agree that he was also aware that death would be a stepping stone to a new risen life, because the work of the Messiah was to inaugurate a new kingdom. Death and resurrection were certainly not what people had been led to expect of their Messiah. Jesus's predictions of his own death and resurrection on the third day are found in Matthew (12:39–40; 16:21; 17:22–23; 20:18–19; 26:32), in Mark (8:27–31; 9:31–32; 14:28; 14:58), in Luke (9:22; 11:29–30; 18:34), and in John (2:19–22; 16:16–22).

(ii) Many people had repeated meetings with the risen Jesus

Many people became followers of Jesus because of meeting him over a period of forty days after he rose from the dead. Some might say their evidence is less credible because they became believers. The opposite is true. Their evidence shows that something completely unexpected must have happened to cause first-century Jews and then non-Jews to lay down their lives in persecution and martyrdom to assert that:

- although Jesus was crucified, he was in fact the long-awaited Messiah who rose from the dead and has set up the kingdom of God for the whole world;

- although he was fully human, he was in a unique way the Son of God, proved by the fact that he lived, died, was buried and then was raised to a new bodily life.

Despite brutal persecution and for some, martyrdom, followers of Jesus travelled throughout the Roman Empire spreading the news that they had met with Jesus after he rose from the dead.

Paul's writings are very early evidence for the resurrection of Jesus. He was a devout Jew who persecuted and killed the followers of Jesus, until he had a direct encounter with the risen Jesus. Paul changed completely, and a man with one of the greatest human minds spent the rest of his life telling and writing about the fact and implications of Jesus being risen from the dead, and he suffered and died as a martyr for it.

James was the brother of Jesus, and at first Jesus's brothers did not believe in him.[8] After the resurrection, James changed completely and became the leader of Jesus's disciples in Jerusalem. He too laid down his life as a martyr, proclaiming that his brother Jesus had been raised from the dead. The explanation for this astonishing change is given in 1 Corinthians 15:7, that after his resurrection, Jesus appeared to James. Nothing else could explain the change from an unbeliever to a courageous leader of the early church, and a martyr who died for his belief.

Peter isn't always pictured in a flattering way in the gospels. He often lacked faith, he sometimes spoke before thinking, he wasn't very dependable, and he even strongly denied that he knew Jesus when Jesus was arrested. Then we are told in 1 Corinthians 15:5 that Jesus appeared to Peter. What else could explain Peter becoming the fearless leader who spent the rest of his life telling people that Jesus is alive and is Lord of all? Peter wrote in 1 Peter 1:3 that we have a living hope through the resurrection of Jesus from the dead. Peter too gave his life for his belief in the risen Jesus during the persecution of Christians in the reign of the emperor Nero.

Paul speaks of many other followers of Jesus in 1 Corinthians 15:6 and says that he appeared to more than five hundred people who saw with their own eyes that Jesus was alive in bodily form after his resurrection, and their lives were completely changed.

There have been various attempts to explain that those who gave their lives for their belief in the risen Jesus may have been deceived. Some claim that the disciples hallucinated. But hallucinations involving not just sight but also speech and touch are very unusual, and for more than five hundred people to share the same hallucination at the same time stretches credulity beyond the limit. To suggest that people at the time of Jesus didn't know the difference between a vision and a real-world meeting is an insult to their intelligence. The great writings of Greek and Roman times demonstrate they were not innocents, but people whose intellectual genius can stand alongside anything we can offer today.

Others claim that the disciples couldn't cope with losing their Messiah after devoting several years of their lives to him and losing everything when he died. Because of this, they came to believe he was alive again. Everything

8. Barth, *Come Holy Spirit*, 299

that happened afterwards shows the weakness of this theory. They spent the rest of their lives proclaiming and dying for what they had experienced, with the story of resurrection shared in detail by all of them because all had shared the experience of being eye-witnesses. A conspiracy theory suggests a degree of duplicity and stupidity among Jesus's followers that makes their lifetimes of persecution and martyrdom completely absurd.

(iii) The tomb in which Jesus was buried was empty, and no dead body was ever found

The absence of a body is remarkable evidence for Jesus's resurrection. Producing the body of Jesus would have put an end to claims of resurrection, and you can be sure there were many of those in positions of power in Judaism at the time who would have loved to put an end to this upstart religion that threatened their beliefs and their positions of power and authority.

The religious and political authorities at the time were determined to stamp out the new faith in Jesus with violence, and producing Jesus's body would have ended it before it properly began, and would have shown the claims about Jesus to be nonsense.

There have been no convincing explanations for the empty tomb and the absence of a dead body. Some claim that Jesus did not die on the cross and woke up in the tomb, but Roman soldiers were not amateurs and Roman crucifixion was brutal, horrific and certainly lethal. It was not an experience to wake up from and start walking around appearing to people.

(iv) There was no ongoing burial site for Jesus, despite its importance in Jewish tradition

The absence of a tomb containing the body of Jesus is also remarkable. The tomb of a leader is an extremely important feature throughout history, and Jewish burial required a twofold process: placing the body in a tomb, and after decomposition, placing the bones in an ossuary. Early Christians had no interest in a tomb or an ossuary because the body of Jesus was no longer dead.

Mark's gospel tells us they knew where he had been laid,[9] but the place had no further relevance. Peter later contrasted the patriarch David

9. Mark 15:47

who died and was buried and whose tomb could be visited, with Jesus who had no such place to visit.[10]The simple fact was that there was no tomb because there was no body to preserve.

Some claim that Jesus's body was buried in some other pit or tomb and never discovered. But Jewish custom required carrying out the burial with great care and ritual and a large number of people would certainly have known exactly where the tomb was. This claim also does nothing to challenge the many reports of those who met the risen Jesus.

Others suggest that Jesus's body was stolen. In Matthew 28:11–15, Roman soldiers were paid to try to put down the claims of resurrection by telling people that the disciples stole the body. But this makes nonsense of the disciples giving their lives and dying as martyrs for the claim he had risen and they had met him. If someone else stole the body, the appearances to so many people are inexplicable.

None of these explanations provides any sensible answer to the empty tomb and the absence of a body which could have shown the world that Jesus was still dead. As Wright explains in his book, *The Resurrection of the Son of God,* the coming together of the empty tomb and the numerous meetings with the risen Jesus provides the strongest evidence for the resurrection. An empty tomb alone would just be a mystery, but there were meetings that followed the resurrection and these were verified by the absence of a dead body.[11]

(v) The written accounts of Jesus's resurrection were based on reports from eye-witnesses

The four gospels of Matthew, Mark, Luke and John were almost certainly written between 50 and 100AD. This was between twenty and seventy years after the events they describe, while contemporaries of Jesus were still alive. Such closeness to the events being described is remarkable in early historical records.

Eye-witness primary sources include the gospels of Matthew, Mark, Luke and John, Luke's book of Acts, the letters of Paul and the letters of Peter. Many of the records of Jesus's resurrection were written at a time when the eye-witnesses were still alive. At first, the news was spread orally. As the church grew and spread out geographically through the Roman empire,

10. Acts 2:9–31

11. Wright, *The Resurrection,* ch.18

it became clear that a written record was needed, and it took time for the gospel writers to collect all they needed from their various sources.

All these early records were written by eye-witnesses or based on eye-witness accounts. Mark used Peter, and Luke worked with Paul, and knew the other apostles and probably Mary the mother of Jesus.[12] Matthew and John are clearly eye-witness based. Peter was present all the time with Jesus, and Paul was closely involved with the Jerusalem apostles and is very clear about his eye-witness credentials.[13] Luke begins his gospel by telling us there are many other earlier eye-witness records.[14] These primary sources have been handed down to us today with remarkable consistency. Some say we have nearly six thousand surviving manuscripts in Greek and thousands in a variety of other ancient languages.[15]

The fact that some details differ from gospel to gospel is confirmation of their dependence on eye-witness accounts rather than carefully crafted, collaborative attempts, sometimes called collusion, to make every detail agree. Evidence for the dependability of the four resurrection accounts includes:

- the complete dependence on individual eye-witness accounts;

- the refusal to airbrush small inconsistencies that might occur with any two or more witnesses of an event;

- the ordinariness of the description, without the spectacular language that often accompanies outlandish descriptions;

- the importance given to the testimony of women whose evidence would have been less acceptable than that of a man in the 1st century AD.

C. S. Lewis claimed that the critic who couldn't distinguish between the historicity of the gospels and the tradition of legends, myths and romances, simply hasn't learnt how to read. In his essay defending the reliable historicity of the gospels, "Fern-Seed and Elephants," he described critics who doubted their historicity as people who claim to be able to see a tiny fern-seed yet can't see an elephant ten yards away in broad daylight. His point was that as a globally recognized expert in the literary genres of

12. Senz, *St. Luke*

13. 1 Cor 9:1 & 15:8

14. Licona, *What are the Primary Sources?*

15. Burroughs, *The Resurrection Accurately Recorded*

myth and legend, he was well equipped to tell the difference between those genres and reliable history.

(vi) Many eye-witnesses and other followers suffered terrible deaths for their belief in Jesus and his resurrection

Many of the early followers of Jesus were willing to suffer great persecution and be killed for the sake of the truth about Jesus's resurrection. They became the foundation of a worldwide church with two and a half billion members today. They made the first day of the week, the day Jesus rose from the dead, their special day to meet and worship, and this remains today with the day we call Sunday.

There's no other explanation for a group of people disillusioned by Jesus's crucifixion turning into followers who travelled the Roman Empire telling the good news that God raised Jesus from the dead. They met opposition in many places from authorities who saw their own power-base threatened.

Here's Paul's description of what he went through because of his determination to spread the news that Jesus was raised from the dead: "I have worked much harder, been in prison more frequently, been flogged more severely, and been exposed to death again and again. Five times I received from the Jews the forty lashes minus one. Three times I was beaten with rods, once I was pelted with stones, three times I was shipwrecked, I spent a night and a day in the open sea, I have been constantly on the move. I have been in danger from rivers, in danger from bandits, in danger from my fellow Jews, in danger from Gentiles; in danger in the city, in danger in the country, in danger at sea; and in danger from false believers. I have labored and toiled and have often gone without sleep; I have known hunger and thirst and have often gone without food; I have been cold and naked."[16]

We know that near the end of his life, Paul was arrested in Caesarea in northern Palestine, and taken to court, where he appealed to Caesar, as was his right as a Roman citizen through his family background. He was taken to Rome and held in house arrest for two years awaiting appearance before the emperor Nero. That's where Luke's account in the book of Acts ends,[17] but the most common view is that Paul may have been executed

---

16. 2 Cor 11:23–27

17. Acts 28:11–31

in the persecution of Christians following the great fire of Rome in 64AD, when a large part of the city was destroyed.

Paul was just one example of the experience of persecution and suffering and martyrdom involved in bringing to the world of the Roman Empire, the good news of the resurrection of Jesus and the new kingdom he established. You needed to be an eye-witness or hear the evidence of eye-witnesses to go through all of that to spread the astonishing news that death is not the end of human life and hope.

(vii) The fast growth of the Christian church would never have happened without Jesus's resurrection

The growth of the Christian church throughout the world did not begin to happen before Jesus was crucified and rose again. It would never have grown beyond a few followers, and would quickly have passed away unnoticed, if Jesus had been crucified and remained dead.

The message that changed the world is clear. "If you confess with your mouth that Jesus is Lord, and believe in your heart that God raised Him from the dead, you will be saved," wrote Paul.[18] The early Christians called the world to a living hope through the resurrection of Jesus Christ from the dead.[19] They were prepared to suffer persecution throughout the Roman empire and to die cruel deaths for one reason: many had personally witnessed the risen Jesus and their eye-witness accounts changed the world.

(viii) Early Christian writers saw the resurrection as the event that changed everything

Early Christian writers are clear that the resurrection of Jesus is the crucial event that changes everything. Clement of Rome, Polycarp, Ignatius, Aristedes, and Justin Martyr are just some of the early writers who make frequent references to the resurrection event.

The writings of Clement of Rome and Polycarp deserve to be called primary sources for Jesus's resurrection, because they knew and benefited from the eye-witness accounts of apostles and other followers of Jesus still alive at the time they were writing. Clement, bishop of Rome from 88 to

18. Rom 10:9

19. 1 Pet 1:3

99AD, was executed under Roman emperor Trajan and had known apostles Peter and John. Polycarp was bishop of Smyrna, and had become a follower of Christ through his relationship with John and other apostles. He was later burned at the stake around 155AD for refusing to burn incense to emperor Antoninus. These two leaders were early examples of those who served and were martyred for their commitment to Jesus and his resurrection.[20]

(ix) Non-Christian writers commented on the new religion based on resurrection

We don't have many surviving references to this new religion in the writings of early non-Christian historians. Palestine was a minor province in the Roman empire and events surrounding the short ministry of someone claiming to be the Jewish Messiah were not high on the Roman Empire's agenda. "Son of god" was one of the titles of the Roman emperor and it would hardly have been prudent to broadcast news about an obscure Jewish prophet claiming that title.[21] As well as that, the destruction of Jerusalem by the Romans in 70AD may have meant the loss of what might have been recorded. Some non-Christian writings do remain and show that belief in the divinity of Jesus was the central conviction of the early Christians.[22]

Roman politician Pliny tells us about Christians regarding Jesus as a god and partaking of a special meal to honour him on a fixed day, presumably celebrating the resurrection.[23] Roman historian Tacitus claims that emperor Nero blamed the great fire in Rome in 64AD on Christians because of their deadly superstition. Historian Gaius Suetonius confirms this, calling the Christian belief a "new and mischievous superstition."[24]

The Jewish religious text, The Talmud, tells of the execution of Yeshua, and it's not surprising that no reference is made to resurrection in a text representing traditional Judaism that had rejected Jesus and tried to put an end to his influence. Jewish historian Josephus has a reference to Jesus appearing to his followers on the third day after his death, but his

---

20. Licona, *What are the Primary Sources?*

21. Wright, *The Resurrection*, ch.20

22. Gleghorn, *Ancient Evidence for Jesus*

23. Pliny the Younger, Letters 10.96.1–7

24. Suetonius, *Life of Nero,* 16.11–13

enthusiasm for Jesus makes some suspect a Christian copyist has embellished his account.[25]

(x) The lives of billions of people have been transformed by their encounter with the risen Jesus

The final and very important piece of evidence for the resurrection of Jesus is personal experience of a life-changing encounter with him. Jesus's resurrection was never meant to be just an interesting historical event, but the wonderful way for God to transform individual lives and through them, life on earth.

What does "encounter with Jesus" mean? The New Testament uses all kinds of ways to help us to understand. The picture of entering through a door is used to emphasize both how much Jesus wants to meet with us, and also the need for us to want to meet with him. In the book of Revelation, the picture is of Jesus standing at the door of our lives and knocking, and if anyone opens the door, he will come in and be with us.[26] In other words, God is always looking for us and wanting to communicate with us. What we need to do is to recognize how much we are loved by God and invite him to share our lives.

In John's gospel, the picture changes. Jesus said "I am the door. Whoever enters by me will be saved."[27] Encounter means a desire to find the truth and a willingness to do some searching, such as giving the story of Jesus a chance by reading it, asking questions, following up what we find and trusting the one who gave his life to rescue us.

I mentioned earlier Karl Barth's explanation of faith as "the gift of the meeting in which we become free to hear the word of grace which God has spoken in Jesus Christ."[28] If the story of Jesus means anything, it means he desires to give us that gift of a meeting: "I have come that you may have life and have it abundantly."[29] That's the ultimate proof of the living presence of Jesus, not as some imaginary subjective experience, but as a real meeting with the Jesus who rose from the dead.

---

25. Josephus, *Description of Jesus*

26. Rev 3:20

27. John 10:9

28. Barth, *Dogmatics in Outline*

29. John 10:10

3. What process might our resurrection take?

N. T. Wright has given an interesting suggestion about resurrection, based on what we know of the bodily resurrection of Jesus. He suggests a waiting stage after death in the presence of God that he calls paradise, while we await the return of Jesus to this earth to raise us to a new bodily life and complete God's new creation. He writes of how Jesus's resurrection is the evidence of God's plan not to abandon this world, but to remake it.[30]

4. If Jesus is Emmanuel (God with us), why did he not come earlier?

In his letter to the Galatians, Paul claims that "when the fullness of the time came, God sent forth his Son."[31] It may well be that "the fullness of time" relates to a stage when humanity was ready, culturally, socially and spiritually, for the coming of Jesus to change the whole pattern of human history and begin what he called his new worldwide kingdom.

Brian Arnold, President of Phoenix Seminary, provides a helpful summary.[32] A context of relative peace, Roman technology, and Greek culture and language may well have helped provide a situation where the gospel of the kingdom, and the reasons why humanity needs it, could be understood and propagated better than at any other time. This might have been the time when the desire for a messiah who would set humanity free reached its most opportune time.

5. How might our present material world connect with God's new earth?

The consistent theme in the Bible is continuity between our work in the present and the new heaven and new earth that is to come when Jesus returns to complete the establishment of his kingdom. Isaiah's vision of the new creation in chapter 65 of his book is completely physical and material, and sets the pattern for Old and New Testament apocalyptic language.[33]

---

30. Wright, *Surprised by Hope*, 293
31. Gal 4:4
32. Gal 4:4
33. Isa 65:17–25

Revelation chapters 21 and 22 present a similar vision of the new Jerusalem. The new earth is the place where "God's dwelling place is now among the people, and he will dwell with them."[34] The description, like Isaiah's, is thoroughly physical and material.

The consistent message of the New Testament is God's restoration and renewal of all things rather than any suggestion of the complete destruction of a present hopeless world in a state of terminal decline. The picture is one of continuity rather than discontinuity between the world we live in now and the new world to come when Jesus returns. This has huge implications for how we see our lives and the task of building the kingdom of God here and now. We don't fall into the pessimism of seeing the world on its way to appointed annihilation, with nothing we can do to save it. Even worse, some think it's good to hasten it on its way to destruction.

Making the world a better place and holding a proper theology of the environment and climate change is building for the future. We work to respect, protect and develop God's creation because Jesus will return in the future to complete the task we've been given to share in the building of God's kingdom of love, goodness, beauty and healing.

If our present world is to be restored and renewed, then we need to explain one New Testament passage in Peter's second letter that seems to give a different picture. Peter writes of how "the elements will be destroyed by fire, and the earth and everything done in it will be burnt up," before the coming of "a new heaven and a new earth, where righteousness dwells."[35] Daniel Wallace, in his note on the textual problem in 2 Peter 3:10, provides good reasons for seeing these verses as referring to the consistent biblical picture of the purifying function of fire to burn up all that is corrupted, leaving a newly refined creation.[36]

Wallace points out that recently discovered manuscripts don't use the Greek word in 2 Peter 3:10 for "burnt up" (*katakaisetai*), but instead the Greek word meaning "laid bare" (*heurethesetai*). That should help us not to see Peter's writing in the context of a Platonic rejection of the material world, or a Stoic belief that the material world will be annihilated by fire. In his first letter, Peter wrote about "the refiner's fire" as God's purifying

34. Rev 21:3
35. 2 Pet 3:10–13
36. Wallace, *A Brief Note*

method.[37] He likened the destruction of the earth to the impact of Noah's flood, which was seen as an act of purification at a time when evil was rampant.[38]

Peter's context is the traditional biblical one in which the "new heaven and new earth" are seen as renewal in continuity with the present material and physical universe. Jesus's resurrected body set the pattern for Christian understanding of material continuity between the present and the future. The transformation that leads us into the future is best summed up in Paul's words in Romans chapter 8: "The creation itself will be liberated from its bondage to decay and brought into the freedom and glory of the children of God."[39]

Further Discussion

1. If you had to pick the best piece of evidence for Jesus's resurrection, what would it be?

2. Do you think the evidence for Jesus's resurrection has the degree of certainty that historians need in order to say that a past event is reliably true?

3. Do you agree that if we find the evidence for the resurrection reliable as a historical event, then we have to ask what that means for our individual lives?

4. Is it a mistake to think that the primary sources for Jesus's resurrection are less reliable because they're all found together in the Bible.

37. 1 Pet 1:6–7 & Mal 3:2
38. 2 Pet 2:5
39. Rom 8:21–22

Chapter 7

The New Creation
Universal Restoration

1. What is the promise of a new creation?

2. What's the good news?

3. Is judgment part of God's restorative process?

4. What does the New Testament say about universal restoration?

5. How has universal restoration been understood in the past?

6. Doesn't the Bible teach about eternal punishment and separation from God?

7. What's the meaning of election?

8. Does universal restoration remove motivation for evangelism?

9. What do we mean by heaven?

10. What do we mean by hell?

11. Is the truth about the universe glorious or tragic?

1. What is the promise of a new creation?

God's promise of a new creation has several aspects to it in the Bible. First, it refers to all who commit to follow Jesus and whose lives are transformed by God's Spirit, as they live with Christ as their Savior and Lord. Paul puts it like this: "if anyone is in Christ, the new creation has come: The old has gone, the new is here."[1] Second, it refers to the work of all disciples of Jesus to contribute to making the world a place where the Lord's Prayer becomes real: "your kingdom come, your will be done, on earth as it is in heaven."[2]

Third, it refers to what Jesus will one day return to complete, what Isaiah prophesied, what the apostle Peter said he was looking forward to, and what John the writer of Revelation saw: "Then I saw a new heaven and a new earth, for the first heaven and the first earth had passed away."[3] There will be no distinction any longer between heaven and earth, when God's loving presence and purposes will oversee everyone and everything. This is not some disembodied state, but the new creation is a "new earth."

In his book, *Do I Stay Christian?* Brian McLaren insists that the work of God's new creation is the completion of what Jesus came to bring: "not an evacuation plan to heaven, but a transformation plan for earth" so that we follow Jesus's example and help people to become "loving human beings who build loving societies." He goes on to say that it's time for Christians "to get serious about our prime directive."

One word that the Bible uses to describe the new creation is the Greek word for universal restoration, "apokatastasis." The concept of universal restoration is quite common in the New Testament, but the actual word "apokatastasis" is used only once, in Peter's second speech to the crowds after the Day of Pentecost. Peter told them that "Jesus must remain in heaven until the time for universal restoration, as God promised long ago through his holy prophets."[4] Peter was claiming that the recent death, resurrection and ascension of Jesus was the fulfilment of all Jewish Messianic hopes, and that Jesus would one day return to complete what we are called to work towards, the restoration of the world to become the perfect kingdom of God on earth.

For the Old Testament prophets, restoration usually referred to their national kingdom with its land and temple. The prophet Ezekiel is interesting because he pays little attention to the issue of land. His main focus is a renewed temple after the Babylonian exile, as the place where Yahweh dwells. The prophets were sure that the promise to Abraham, "through your

---

1. 2 Cor 5:17
2. Matt 6:10
3. 2 Cor 5:17, Matt 6:10, Rev 21:1
4. Acts 3:21 (NRSVue)

offspring all nations on earth will be blessed,"[5] would be the outcome of the messianic restoration.

People have different ideas about what universal restoration means, so let me begin with some general statements about it, that we might be able to agree on.

- The good news of the gospel is found in the life, death and resurrection of Jesus. Everything we hold about the present and the future is based on how Jesus has transformed human history, and has provided our hope for the future.

- When John writes in his first letter that "God is love," he tells us that love is the very essence of God's being and characterizes all God is and does.[6]

- The New Testament develops God's promise of "a new heaven and a new earth"[7] in which all will be restored and renewed. The building of God's new creation has started now and will be completed when Jesus returns.

- Justice tempered with mercy, exercised with complete fairness and wisdom, is a universal moral standard, and is what we hope for from God. We recognize that God's perfect love and holiness must be outraged by human greed and the cruelty inflicted on men, women and children, together with the whole animal world, throughout human history.

- We find warnings and examples of God's judgment in the Bible, but as John Oswalt writes in his commentary on the book of Isaiah, "judgment is never God's last word, but his intention is to use judgment to bring about lasting hope."[8] The constant biblical theme is that everything God does has a positive purpose and outcome.

Paul's claim that "God's purpose is to unite all things in Jesus, everything in heaven and everything on earth"[9] is repeated many times in the New Testament, constantly using words like "all" and "every" to emphasize

---

5. Gen 22:18

6. 1 John 4:16

7. Rev 21:1. See also Isa 65:17 and 2 Pet 3:13

8. Oswalt, *The NIV Application Commentary: Isaiah*, 43

9. Eph 1:10

the inclusivity of the love of God, or as Thomas Talbott calls it, "the inescapable love of God."[10]

2. What's the good news?

The German philosopher, Schopenhauer, is famous for his bleak outlook on life. He began his essay *On the Suffering of the World* with a warning that we shouldn't imagine there's a meaning to life, unless we happen to believe that our purpose in being here is to suffer. When we see a world filled with war, famine and pain, we can maybe have some sympathy with Schopenhauer's bleak pessimism.

The strange thing about Christianity is that the cruel murder of its founder led to his followers going throughout the world with what they called the "gospel," a word meaning "good news." What could bring good news to a world filled with pain and suffering? The last thing our world needs is well-meaning wishful thinking to help us cope with reality. That's why N. T. Wright, in *Simply Good News*, insists that the good news is not good advice about how to live. It's about life-changing events that have already happened in the birth, life, death and resurrection of Jesus.[11] These events have changed everything about human life, and those who come to understand this find their lives utterly transformed.

That's why the early followers of Jesus travelled the known world, calling on people everywhere to come into a relationship with the risen Jesus, and commit themselves to get to know him and follow him. This gave people everywhere the opportunity to be part of God's work of making all things new, getting God's new world under way, doing what Jesus had done, loving and supporting all, especially the poor, the weak, the oppressed, and the suffering.

Spending time with Jesus when he rose after three days in the grave gave his followers absolute confidence in their good news, and they taught that Jesus will return one day and establish a new earth, where the heaven of God's presence and the earth of human life become one. This restoration is already under way in the new kingdom Jesus has established. Our hope of heaven is an experience and task here and now.

Because the world is set in one direction only, towards God's ultimate purpose of renewal and restoration of all things, then living for oneself,

10. Talbott, *The Inescapable Love of God*
11. Wright, *Simply Good News* ch.1

just for one's own pleasure and profit, is doomed to be missing the whole point of human existence. The repeated promise of "a new heaven and a new earth," in which all will be restored and renewed[12] refers to a complete coming together of the present heaven (where God's loving goodness and purity control all things), and the earthly life of God's creation.

3. Is judgment part of God's restorative purpose?

It would be arrogant to claim that we know answers about how God chooses to act in overseeing the created universe, but we can use things we know for sure about God, and explore, investigate and speculate on the basis of the evidence we have.

One starting point is clear. John tells us that "God is love,"[13] and the great demonstration of that is the life, the death, and the resurrection of Jesus, as well as the day-to-day experience of his presence in all of life's circumstances. Love is so important that Psalm 136 repeats it 26 times: "God's love endures for ever." Paul develops that fundamental truth. "Neither life nor death . . . nor anything else in all creation will be able to separate us from the love of God in Christ Jesus our Lord."[14] It is Jesus who has made visible the truth that "God is love," now and forever.

We can also be sure about God's insistence on justice. The psalmists and the prophets spoke of God's condemnation of abuses of power, for "you, God, see the trouble of the afflicted; you consider their grief and take it in hand. The victims commit themselves to you; you are the helper of the fatherless."[15] "Learn to do right; seek justice. Defend the oppressed"[16] was the call of Isaiah. We can also recognize that God's love and care are for the whole created universe, and not just for humans. We are part of the story, but restoration involves all that God has made.

It's not surprising that there are objections to the idea of universal restoration. Isn't the Bible full of very severe warnings about judgment? How does universal restoration sit alongside the appalling evil, brutality and corruption that human beings have committed and inflicted on others throughout history? For some people, the greatest problem with an

12. Isa 65:17 & 66:22, 2 Pet 3:13, Rev 21:1–5
13. 1 John 4:16
14. Rom 8:38–39
15. Ps 10:14
16. Isa 1:17

all-inclusive, universal restoration is that it offends their sense of justice. This would be true if we failed to take into account divine judgment. We can't ignore the warning in the book of Hebrews that "it's a dreadful thing to fall into the hands of the living God."[17] Jesus often warned that judgment is inevitable if we reject his teaching about God's love and holiness. Justice requires taking responsibility for our choices and their impact.

We do not know what form God's justice and judgment might take. The warnings are clear, but we shouldn't think that God's justice is similar to the human desire for revenge. The difference between God's justice and our human understanding of retribution is seen in Paul's call to the Christians in Rome not to look for revenge for abusive treatment, but to leave it to God.[18] Paul quotes an Old Testament verse from The Song of Moses in Deuteronomy where Moses warns that justice and judgment belong to God because "vengeance is mine, I will repay."[19] Moses called on his people to know that God's justice would come, and the very next verse assures them of God's mercy when people see the folly of their ways.

Paul's point is that we should leave our desire for recompense to God, and he follows that immediately with the call of Jesus himself. "If your enemy is hungry, feed him. If he is thirsty, give him something to drink." Vengeance in God's hands will be productive and restorative, and has none of the human desire for revenge.

Justice is an integral part of God's love, and always serves a divine purpose. A. W. Tozer explains it well: "nothing God ever does, or ever did, or ever will do, is separate from the love of God."[20] The message of the Bible shows that the goal of judgment, on this side of death, is often to protect and vindicate the poor, the oppressed, and the victimized. After death, judgment, hugely painful as it is, is part of a process that starts and ends in the loving purpose of God to reform, repair, and ultimately restore and unify in Christ all things in creation.

There's no conflict in the Bible between God's love and mercy and his holiness and justice. God's severity and God's judgment are acts of mercy to deliver us from evil, and it seems clear in the Bible that God's purifying love can take the form of wrath with a redemptive purpose.

17. Heb 10:31
18. Rom 12:19
19. Deut 32:35
20. Tozer, The Attributes of God

Throughout Paul's writings, what connects God's love and God's justice is God's mercy "for God has bound everyone over to disobedience, so that he may have mercy on them all."[21] The connection between judgment and hope runs throughout the Bible. It's the central message of the Old Testament prophets. Isaiah's prophetic message is clear that there is always a positive purpose in judgment.[22]

I mentioned earlier John Oswalt's claim that "judgment is never God's last word." Mark Boda makes the same point in his commentary on the minor prophets. He explains how the words of the prophet Habakkuk resound throughout the Bible: "in your anger, remember mercy."[23] Boda points out that when the prophets speak of God's anger, the context is often the promise of mercy and assistance to follow. He writes of how "a reference to God's anger" produces "the expectation that there will be a turn to something new, that the mercy of God is imminent."[24]

There's an obvious question if the purpose of judgment is to bring about restoration. What's the meaning of salvation through believing in Christ here and now? Salvation is rescue from a terrible situation, in which we receive forgiveness for all the ways in which we fall far short of loving God with all our being, and of loving other people as we love ourselves. Reconciliation with God through the death of Jesus on the cross leads to what Jesus called "life in abundance," lived with the assurance of God's forgiveness here and now, in personal relationship with God now, and in the world to come.[25]

Living with and for God means God's presence in all life's challenges, the daily experience of God's loving care and the gift of meaning and purpose in life. In Paul's words, "there is now no condemnation for those who are in Christ Jesus, because through Christ the law of the Spirit who gives life has set you free from the law of sin and death."[26] Those who deliberately choose to miss out on this, the whole meaning of life, will obviously know immense remorse.

The key point is that judgment and wrath in the Bible are never wholly negative concepts. God is love, and judgment and severity are

21. Rom 11:32
22. Isa 2:1–4
23. Hab 3:2
24. Boda, *Haggai & Zechariah*, 177
25. John 10:10
26. Rom 8:1–2

aspects of purifying love. To lose this constant biblical emphasis leads to a very different, pitiless God like the one in Jonathan Edwards's influential eighteenth-century sermon, "Sinners in the Hands of an Angry God." The idea of everlasting punishment is not only out of all proportion, but it also achieves no outcome. Even as humans we know we should not torture the most monstrous of criminals, because we would sink to their level, and achieve no positive result.

4. What does the New Testament say about universal restoration?

Paul and John both refer to every person and created being joining in worship in the apokatastasis. "At the name of Jesus every knee shall bow, in heaven and on earth and under the earth, and every tongue confess that Jesus Christ is Lord." (Philippians 2:10–11, quoting Isaiah 45:23). "Then I heard every creature in heaven and on earth and under the earth and in the sea, and all that is in them, saying: 'to him who sits on the throne and to the Lamb be praise and honour and glory and power for ever and ever.'" (Revelation 5:13). Some commentators see it as enforced, unwilling confession, but it must be far more real and more wonderful than that. All will eventually take part in the worship due to the divine Trinity.

When Jesus tells us in John's gospel, "I, when I am lifted up from the earth, will draw all people to myself,"[27] his statement alerts us never to underestimate what he would achieve through the cross, for it would lead to the bringing in of God's new creation. A better translation of John 12:32 would be "I, when I am lifted up from the earth, will draw all to myself," for the object of "draw" is *pantas* (the object form of *pas* in Greek), simply meaning "all." Adding the word "people" is probably because John has just told us that many Greeks were listening to him, having come to Jerusalem for the Passover festival.

When Paul shares his excitement in his letters, he often uses the words "all" and "everything in heaven and everything on earth" to emphasize how inclusive the restoration will be. "God's purpose is to unite all things in Jesus, everything in heaven and everything on earth." (Ephesians 1:10). "Through him to reconcile to himself all things, everything on earth and everything in heaven, making peace through his blood on the cross."

27. John 12:32

(Colossians 1:19–20). It would be strange if this meant everything but excluded the people.

In the other New Testament quotations below, seeing "all" as sometimes meaning "potentially all" is possible, but the all-inclusive nature of God's loving purposes shines through:

- "As in Adam all die, so in Christ all will be made alive." (1 Corinthians 15:22)

- "Just as one trespass resulted in condemnation for all people, so one righteous act resulted in justification and life for all people." (Romans 5:18)

- "God has bound everyone over to disobedience, so that he may have mercy on them all." (Romans 11:32)

- "We are convinced that one died for all, and therefore all died." (2 Corinthians 5:14)

- "God wants all people to be saved, and come to a knowledge of the truth." (1 Timothy 2:4)

- "The living God is the savior of all people, especially of those who believe." (1 Timothy 4:10)

- "The grace of God has appeared bringing salvation to all." (Titus 2:11)

- "Christ is the atoning sacrifice for our sins and not only for ours, but also for the sins of the whole world." (1 John 2:2)

5. How has universal restoration been understood in the past?

Confidence in restoration of all things was common in the early centuries of church history.[28] Salvation was often seen as cosmic and universal, for this is the precise meaning of Christ's victory. There are no limits to God's plan to renew and restore, and it's all founded on what Jesus has achieved through his life, death and resurrection.

Paul describes reconciliation between us and God as "making peace through Christ's blood on the cross."[29] When he writes in Philippians that

28. Kimel, *The Universalist Hope*

29. Col 1:20

"every knee shall bow and every tongue confess that Jesus Christ is Lord,"[30] he is quoting Isaiah 45:23 where Yahweh says that ultimately everyone will bow and every tongue swear allegiance to Him. Paul is saying that the same worship will be given to Jesus by all created beings. The only foundation for such a reconciliation is the victory of the cross. To doubt the ultimate universality of God's gracious restoration of all is to underestimate the power of Christ's sacrifice.

In the 4th century, Roman emperor Constantine decided a clear, agreed theology was needed and the influence of imperial politics of power and control came to the fore. The Western church from the 5th century onwards has tended to follow the teaching of Augustine, Bishop of Hippo in North Africa during Constantine's imperialization of Christianity. The emphasis on an all-loving God whose mercy extends to all lost its pre-eminence. As Richard Rohr writes, in contrast to the Eastern church, "the Western church went down the road of a very limited victory for God."[31]

The Second Council of Constantinople in the year 553 condemned apokatastasis as a heresy, showing how much the teachings of early church fathers, such as Justin Martyr, Clement of Alexandria, Origen and Gregory of Nyssa, were a challenge to this new imperial age. The biblical emphasis on "all" and "everything" developed into an emphasis on "some" (the elect) and "a few" (those who will be saved). An understanding of salvation in which fear of ultimate damnation became central was followed by a long history of brutal persecution of all considered heretics. A message of fear requires the weapons of fear to defend it.[32]

In her 14th century book, *Revelations of Divine Love*, Julian of Norwich, living through the Hundred Years War and the Black Death and her own sickness and pain, recorded hearing God say the words: "All shall be well . . . and all manner of things shall be well."[33] Recording the sixteen visions God had given her, she struggled to reconcile her revelations of God's love, the motherhood of God revealed in Christ, and the promise that "all shall be well," with the teachings of Holy Church about the sufferings of the damned.

---

30. Phil 2:10–11 and Isa 45:23

31. Rohr, *The Early Eastern Church*

32. Scott & Sadie, *The Restoration*

33. Julian of Norwich, *Revelations of Divine Love*, 74–78

That remained a puzzle that she couldn't answer, but the one thing she knew is that God will make well all that is not well. Her confidence wasn't a statement of selfishness (all will be well for me, or just for some of us), nor was it a claim of foolish idealism. What she held as certainty was the promised renewal of all things, brought about by the sufferings and victory of Jesus on the cross.

6. Doesn't the Bible teach about eternal punishment and separation from God?

Let's look at the four main New Testament examples that are often taken as indicating separation from God after death, either into non-existence, or into "eternal punishment" of some kind.

(i) Eternal fire

Mention of the punishment of "eternal fire" occurs three times in the New Testament. In Matthew 18:8, it's in the context of abusive behaviour towards children. Jesus shows his horror by saying it's better to cut off an offending limb now that be thrown into eternal fire later. In Matthew 25:41, the context is failure to care for the hungry, the thirsty, the sick, the poor, the stranger and the prisoner. The punishment is eternal fire. In Jude 7, Sodom and Gomorrah suffer eternal fire because of their wicked behaviour. There's a case for saying that in all three verses we have an unwarranted translation from the original text of the word "eternal," and that we can misunderstand the word "fire."

The adjective translated "eternal" in all three verses is *aionios* in Greek. It comes from the noun *aion*, meaning an age, a certain period of time. *Aionios* therefore means "for a length of time," and can be used about the past, the present or the future. *Aionios* is the word Paul uses in Romans 16:24, when he says that the gospel is the mystery which was kept secret "for a long time in the past." *Aion* is the word Paul uses in Romans 12:2 when he tells us not to be conformed to "the age" in which we live. Jesus uses it to describe the people of "this age" in Luke 20:34.

When it's used about the future, it's properly translated as "in the age to come."[34] There's no implication of endlessness. In fact, it implies a lim-

---

34. New Catholic Encyclopedia, *Aeon in the Bible*

ited period. Translating the word *aionios* as "eternal" or "everlasting" adds an unwarranted idea of never-ending punishment to the original biblical text, which says it's something that will happen "in the age to come."[35]

In the Bible, fire is most often a metaphor for cleansing and purifying through a necessarily painful process. God's messenger in the book of Malachi is "like a refiner's fire." He will "purify . . . and refine . . . like gold and silver."[36] As Gregory MacDonald points out, in Revelation chapter 19, the kings of the earth are cast into the lake of fire but then, presumably purified, in Revelation 21 they enter the new Jerusalem.[37] The reference to Sodom as having suffered "eternal fire," doesn't negate Ezekiel's prophecy that "God will restore the fortunes of Sodom,"[38] or Jesus's own claim that judgment on Sodom would be "more tolerable" than judgment on the towns that rejected him as Israel's Messiah.[39]

Going through a time of painful cleansing for wrongdoing always has the goal of bringing restoration and renewal. We're not surprised that Jesus should be so angry about child abuse, but we can take note of his anger about out failure to care for the poor and others in need. God is love, and experiencing God's love as a consuming, purifying fire[40] will no doubt make weeping and gnashing of teeth a way of describing the response. The process of coming to understand sinfulness is also called falling into outer darkness.[41] The judgment of experiencing the emptiness of separation from God may be the only way to come to restoration.

(ii) The story of the sheep and the goats

The context of Jesus's story about the sheep and the goats in Matthew's gospel is clearly what we do here and now for the needy.[42] The sheep are those who "see you hungry and feed you . . . see you a stranger and welcome you . . . see you sick or in prison and visit you." Jesus could hardly put more

35. Talbott, *The Inescapable Love*, 83

36. Mal 3: 2–3

37. MacDonald, *The Evangelical Universalist*, 116

38. Ezek 16:53

39. Matt 11:24

40. Heb 12:29

41. Matt 8:12

42. Matt 25:31–46

strongly and compellingly the anger of God when we act as the goats and do none of those acts of care and compassion.

In looking at some of the stories referred to here, I'm grateful to Thomas Talbott's *The Inescapable Love of God*, where he examines them in detail.[43] In the story of the sheep and the goats, the Greek word used for punishment is *kolasis*, whose established meaning referred to the pruning of trees. God's punishment is always in the interest of the one who suffers it. It isn't spoken of in terms of the Greek word for revenge (*timoria*), which is in the interest of the one who inflicts it. Punishment is corrective, whereas revenge is not, and it is in keeping with all we learn about God that all he does is creative and productive.

(iii) The story of the rich man and Lazarus

On another occasion, Jesus used a well-known Jewish folktale about a rich man and Lazarus, to show that if people ignore the teaching of the prophets about care for the poor, then not even a supernatural event would reach them.[44] Jesus uses the folk-tale to warn the rich that they will suffer the agony of fire if they refuse to help the poor in need of aid.

The picture of the rich man and Lazarus in the afterlife is a Jewish folk picture that precedes the outcome of Jesus's death and resurrection, but still provides a severe warning of God's judgment on all who fail to care for the needy. Fire is clearly used to signify a just punishment in the age to come, but, as always, it can be educative and restorative.[45]

(iv) Everlasting destruction

In 2 Thessalonians 1:9, Paul tells the church in Thessalonica that punishment will come to those who are persecuting them. Paul's warning about what the persecutors will suffer has sometimes been translated as "everlasting destruction, and shut out from the presence of the Lord." Again, Talbott, in *The Inescapable Love of God*, and MacDonald, in *The Evangelical Universalist*, provide a detailed discussion of this verse.[46]

43. Talbott, *The Inescapable Love of God*, 77–82
44. Hilborn, *The Nature of Hell*, 81
45. Talbott, *The Inescapable Love of God*, 86–88
46. MacDonald, *The Evangelical Universalist*, 150–55

The Greek text of 2 Thessalonians 1:9 is very clear. It tells us that the evildoer will suffer "destruction from (*apo*) the presence of the Lord." The word for "from" is *apo* in Greek. This is the same construction that we find in Acts 3:19 about times of refreshing that will come "from (*apo*) the presence of the Lord."

Some translations of 2 Thessalonians 1:9 have extended this into a paraphrase, adding words like "separated from" or "shut out from" the presence of the Lord, to make the destruction sound more final, but these words don't appear in the original Greek text.

The attempt to give added strength to Paul's warning is unhelpfully intensified by translating the word *aionios* as "everlasting." As we saw earlier, the normal meaning of the word is "for a length of time," and when used about the future, is more properly translated as "in the age to come." In fact, it's quite reasonable to see 2 Thessalonians 1:9 as yet another warning about how painful the corrective and restorative work of God's judgment will be.[47]

7. What's the meaning of election?

The key point about election is that the elected one is elected to serve on behalf of all, and that service often involves great hardship. Someone needs to do it, and that falls to the elected one. In the Bible, election of one (Abraham, Jacob, Joseph etc.) is never rejection of another (Ishmael, Esau). Election is always a calling to bring about the good and ultimate salvation of all, including Ishmael and Esau.

Choosing Jacob rather than Esau didn't change the fact that for Jacob, seeing Esau face to face was "like seeing the face of God."[48] Choosing Isaac rather than Ishmael didn't change the fact that Ishmael was the one to whom God promised "Lift the boy up and take him by the hand, for I will make of him a great nation."[49] Choosing Joseph wasn't in order to elevate him above his brothers. It was so they and the people of Egypt would be rescued from the threat of famine. Restricting God's love and mercy to a chosen few denies everything that the Bible tells us about God and has no place in the Christian gospel.

---

47. Talbott, *The Inescapable Love of God*, 93
48. Gen 33:10
49. Gen 21:18

8. Does universal restoration remove motivation for evangelism?

The message of universal restoration and reconciliation is the greatest possible motivation for mission to the world. It doesn't lessen the drive to evangelize. On the contrary, it adds greater compulsion and urgency to our mission to transform the quality of human life here and now through knowing Christ, and to call everyone to avoid the desolation of having missed the whole purpose of life.

As N. T. Wright explains, God's project is to fill the earth with the life of heaven, which Jesus will return to complete. God calls us to be his co-workers for the restoration of the whole creation, and to extend the kingdom of love, hope, peace and meaning to the world and to the human story.[50] Our mission is to share the message of God's astonishing love bringing hope for all. The good news is that not only has Christ given our lives meaning and purpose with the presence of God's Spirit with us, but the best message of all is, in the words of Thomas Talbott, that "the truth about the universe is ultimately glorious, not tragic."[51]

9. What do we mean by heaven?

The word "heaven" is the common translation of the Hebrew word *shamayim* and the Greek word *ouranos*. Both mean "the heights," and the primary meaning of heaven in the Bible refers to the physical universe beyond the earth, the realm of the sun, moon, and stars, sometimes translated simply as "sky." Heaven then also becomes extended into the realm of non-earthly, transcendent reality that is the realm of God and of non-earthly beings. The word "heaven" can also sometimes be substituted for the name of God, as in the phrase "kingdom of heaven."

Heaven thus comes to mean the context in which God's will is completely operative. Hence the Lord's Prayer: "your will be done on earth as it is in heaven." Earth is the place and context where human will is operative, and where we enjoy degrees of freedom to choose and act, and can make earthly experience heavenly or devilish. All that we experience here and now works to prepare us for the future reality where earth and heaven become fully one. Redemption is cosmic in scope and involves the whole

50. Wright, *Surprised by Hope*, 293

51. Parry, *Universal Salvation?* 265

universe, and the new earth will be a place where the will of God is fully in control.

In *The Groaning of Creation*, Christopher Southgate reminds us that we shouldn't talk about heaven as if only human beings are of concern in the redeeming purposes of God.[52] The whole of creation is to be redeemed. The new creation is the culmination of all that we are involved in here and now, bringing the heaven of God's will to earthly life and experience, until the new earth is established.

Heaven is thus wherever God's will is fully carried out, and it can refer to making our present experience "heavenly" as a foretaste of what is to come in the kingdom of God. The new earth is where our resurrected bodies will experience the completeness of God's will and kingdom.

10. What do we mean by hell?

The word "hell" translates three Greek words. The first, *Hades*, occurs ten times in the New Testament, and refers simply to the abode of the departed spirits of the dead. Thus, when Christ promised to build his church, and the gates of *Hades* would not prevail against it, he proclaimed that the church would share in his victory over death through his resurrection.

The word *tartarus* occurs once in 2 Peter 2:4, and refers to a deep pit with the association of being a place where the wicked dead await judgment.

The word *Gehenna* is found twelve times in the New Testament, eleven of them in the words of Jesus himself. Gehenna is a transliteration of an Old Testament Hebrew expression, "the valley of Hinnom," which was a ravine on the southern side of Jerusalem, used in past times as a place where children were sacrificed to the pagan god Molech. In the time of Jesus, it had become the garbage dump of Jerusalem where there was continual burning of refuse. *Gehenna* thus becomes a metaphor for a reality that has become all too frequent in human history, where the goodness and love of God are displaced by unspeakable cruelty and suffering.

Gehenna also relates to another reality, the educative and restorative judgment of God in the world to come. When Jesus speaks of punishment in relation to Gehenna, the Greek word used is *kolasis*, originally referring to the pruning of trees, and carries the meaning of purging or purifying.

If we use the word "punishment" in relation to God, then it is in the interest of the one who suffers it. Punishment is corrective, whereas

---

52. Southgate, *The Groaning of Creation*, 37

revenge is not. Weeping and gnashing of teeth are a response to corrective experiences.[53] The image of fire in the Bible usually refers to a consuming, purifying power. It's not surprising that Richard Evans called his recent study of Nazi concentration camps *The Anatomy of Hell*. If you make a visit to Auschwitz, you walk around a place of suffering caused by evil that truly deserves to be called a hell. It's shameful if we give the impression that hell is a place of similar or worse suffering to which God assigns people, if they fail to do what he requires.

Appalling torture of prisoners and captured enemies was commonplace in the ancient empires of Persia, Greece and Rome. You would expect things to change for followers of the founder of Christianity who said "love your enemies, do good to those who hate you, bless those who curse you, pray for those who persecute you."[54] However, the use of torture has been carried out in the name of religion throughout history. From the persecution of Jews under Constantine, to Crusades to conquer the Holy Land, horrific Catholic inquisitions, and torture of heretics and non-conformists of all kinds by both Protestants and Catholics in the 16th century, the crimes have continued. Why did we have to wait 18 centuries after the time of Jesus for physical torture to be widely recognized as a crime against humanity? There were voices for universal human rights throughout history before that, but they never became mainstream.

The only answer I can find is that the doctrine of a God-ordained hell with horrible, everlasting punishments became established with the imperialization of Christianity under Constantine. It created an astonishing blindness in people who assumed it was not only possible, but right to inflict torture to punish opposition and wipe out what they saw as heresy or refusal to conform. It became the norm for people to think that this is what God will do, so it is right for us to do the same.

11. Is the ultimate truth about the universe glorious or tragic?[55]

As Christopher Southgate writes, a God of loving relationship never regards any creature as "a mere evolutionary expedient."[56] If death has the last word over the vast majority of people, the victory of Christ is hugely

53. Matt 25:30

54. Matt 5:44, Luke 6:27

55. Thomas Talbott's words in Parry, *Universal Salvation?* 265

56. Southgate, *The Groaning of Creation*, 16

limited. The judgment of God tells us about the severely educative, reformative, and restorative nature of experience in the world to come.

If we were to see justice and judgment as having no corrective and restorative value, it would be very difficult to answer valid questions about God's goodness and love, like the ones below:

- Is there a final outcome that will outweigh the massive weight of pain and suffering throughout the evolutionary process? The final good must outweigh the suffering and destruction experienced in the process of reaching it.

- Is evil an ultimate reality, or does it have a final end? Evil in all its forms and outcomes, including suffering, must have a final end.

- Can we really have fullness of joy and love in heaven while others ultimately remain outside it? Heaven can only be experienced as heaven because we know all evil and suffering will end, and through the process of judgment, all will be included in God's saving grace. We can no more remain happy knowing another has come to a bad end, than remain happy if we come to a bad end ourselves.

- Is anyone or anything left outside the realm of Christ's final victory? Nothing and no-one will remain outside of Christ's victory over sin and evil, and anything less than that underestimates what Jesus has achieved.

- Is God able to bring about his desire that no-one should perish? God will ensure that his plans are fulfilled.

Only the ultimate goal of restoration for all, in a life of perfect consciousness of God in a world beyond this one, means that the conditions of the present have been ultimately worthwhile. God's mission is to restore the whole creation, and our goal here and now is to extend the kingdom of God which brings love, hope, peace and meaning to the world. Christ's atoning death is the only basis on which this forgiveness and new life come about. God's good purpose in judgment allows us to agree with Thomas Talbott and see that the universe doesn't end in disaster and tragedy, but in John's vision of the glorious praise and worship offered by "every creature in heaven and on earth and under the earth and in the sea, and all that is in them."[57]

57. Revelation 5:13

Further Discussion

1. Do you agree with Brian McLaren that the Christian gospel is "not an evacuation plan to heaven," but "a transformation plan for earth"?

2. Do you think it's true that God's judgments always have a positive purpose and outcome?

3. Do you think the "new earth" is a helpful description of heaven?

4. Paul wrote that "God's purpose is to unite all things in Jesus, everything in heaven and everything on earth" (Ephesians 1:10), and "through him to reconcile to himself all things, everything on earth and everything in heaven, making peace through his blood on the cross" (Colossians 1:20). On another occasion, Peter spoke about "the time of universal restoration" (Acts 3:21). Does all of this mean that no-one and nothing will ultimately be excluded?

5. Is Thomas Talbott right to claim that "the ultimate truth about the universe is glorious, not tragic"?

Chapter 8

God and the Meaning of Sovereignty

1. What does "God is in control" mean?

2. What kind of freedom has God given to the creation?

3. Are there limits on freedom?

4. Does God experience changing emotions and journey through time with us?

5. Is the future known to God in his relationship with the creation?

6. But isn't God infinite in wisdom?

7. So, is God in control?

8. Does prayer change things?

1. What does "God is in control" mean?

"God is in control" is a claim we often hear in response to the chaos that seems to govern so much of human life. It's a statement that is made with great confidence, but an explanation of what we mean by it is less clear. If we want to investigate what "God is in control" means, we need to start by emphasizing that this is not a question about who God is. It's a question about how God relates to the universe he has created.

Nor is it a question about the authority of Jesus whose great commission to his disciples began: "All authority in heaven and on earth has been given to me."[1] It's a question about how God uses his sovereignty and how Jesus exercises his authority. We might see a helpful pointer to God's sovereignty and Jesus's authority in his announcement of his mission, to "proclaim good news to the poor . . . to proclaim freedom for the prisoners and recovery of sight for the blind, to set the oppressed free, to proclaim the year of the Lord's favor."[2] In the kingdom of God, power and greatness aren't shown in the methods of human, political leaders. They're shown in love and grace, generosity and forgiveness, service and self-sacrifice.

Let me explain two traditional views about God and control, and then suggest a third, very different way of looking at it.

(i) Theological determinism

There are two traditional assumptions about God and control. Neither seems satisfactory to me. The first traditional view is called theological determinism and believes everything that happens is an outcome of God's will and plan. It's all part of God's great design. Theological determinism plays a strong role in Islam and there are elements of it in Judaism that carry over into Christian theology through influencers like Augustine and Aquinas to Calvin and to the present day.

The problems with theological determinism are obvious. Any suggestion that the God of love whom we meet in the Bible and above all, in Christ, should have any involvement with every kind of cruelty and evil is offensive. It's also a view that leaves no room at all for human freedom to make choices or moral responsibility for our actions.

Those objections to determinism are so clear that a view called soft determinism (also called compatibilism) developed. This claims that when we have two important beliefs that seem contradictory, we hold on to each of them and presumably accept that our human minds are inadequate to integrate them. God pre-ordains everything, but we're still free and responsible. That may sound like a way to get out of a hard situation, but I think many Christians find themselves in that position. They're not really sure what they mean when they say that God is in control, but they're certain that it's true.

1. Matt 28:18
2. Luke 4:18–19

(ii) God allows things to happen

The other traditional and more common view is that whatever happens is because God in his wisdom allows it. God deciding to allow or not allow some terrible event seems an unhelpful picture of the dynamic activity of God, and still leaves God having at least the appearance of some involvement with wicked things that happen. Sometimes a connection is made between God allowing things to happen, and the claim that "all things work together for good for those who love God." That sounds as if God will make sure things turn out well for us, despite the terrible things that happen in the world.

As N. T. Wright and others have pointed out, "all things work together for good for those who love God," is not what Paul is telling us in Romans 8:28. We are not told that God will make sure that things will always work out well for us. Instead, we are the ones being told to be active, and we're assured that God will work with us towards the goal of bringing something good out of every situation. A better translation of the Greek statement is: "God works together with those who love him to bring about good."[3]

(iii) An open view of God at work

Let me try in this chapter to explain an alternative to both of those views. In 1994, five theologians, Clark Pinnock, Richard Rice, John Sanders, William Hasker, and David Basinger, caused a stir with their Inter-Varsity Press book, *The Openness of God: A Biblical Challenge to the Traditional Understanding of God.* It's a summary and defence of what is known as open theology. What the five scholars were suggesting wasn't new. The main idea has always been discussed, but it was important that five renowned theologians were making a thoroughly biblical explication of it, and using the popular IVP to present it.

Open theology focuses on reading the Bible with at least two major questions. First, does the freedom, that is God's gift to us in creation, mean that the future is genuinely open, not pre-ordained or determined by God? Second, in order to make freedom genuinely open, has God willingly and graciously limited his foreknowledge of the future in order to journey with us through life and through time?

---

3. Wright, "The Bible's Most Misunderstood Verse"

2. What kind of freedom has God given to the creation?

In human life, we experience very different degrees of freedom, given the huge number of variables that constrain people's lives. Sadly, our freedom, which can be used to choose to love God and the created world, to serve each other, and to build community, has also been a freedom used to inflict suffering on our fellow human beings, and create barriers for their freedom to choose and to act.

When we think about God's gift of freedom for us to make choices and take responsibility for our actions, we often forget that human freedom can only operate meaningfully if that gift of freedom is also given to the universe in which we live. John Polkinghorne calls it "love's gift of freedom" and freedom for the processes of the cosmos is the essential partner to freedom for human beings.[4] As C. S. Lewis explains in *Mere Christianity*, there's no point in creating a world of automata who cannot take the responsibility of freely choosing to love.[5]

When we speak of God's gift of freedom, we shouldn't have to accept that life on earth can just be collateral damage for so many of God's creatures. Christopher Southgate, writing about the waste and destruction that have been one aspect of the evolutionary process, sets out a relevant principle that a loving God cannot regard any of his creatures as "a mere evolutionary expedient."[6] As Keith Ward writes, "one person's suffering cannot morally be outweighed by another person's flourishing."[7]

Nobel Prize-winning physicist, Steven Weinberg, in his book, *Dreams of a Final Theory*, expresses an understandable response to the death of most of his family in the Holocaust, and asks whether the suffering and death of millions in Nazi concentration camps was the price to pay for other people's freedom to choose.[8] That's a huge question that I've tried to engage with in chapter 3 of this book, "Suffering, Evil, and a God of Love."

4. Polkinghorne, *Science and Providence*, 75–77

5. Lewis, *Mere Christianity*, 48

6. Southgate, *The Groaning of Creation*, 16

7. Ward, *The Big Questions*, 51

8. Weinberg, *Dreams of a Final Theory*

3. Are there limits on freedom?

We know that God has set limits on the freedom given to our world. One is the natural laws that provide parameters within which the universe operates. God's faithfulness to the laws of nature, a consistency that makes science possible, means if he chooses to override the laws of nature, there is a special purpose.

The second limitation on freedom is that God will always be able to intervene and ensure that his ultimate purposes will be fulfilled. The Bible records many prophecies about outcomes that are part of God's plans for the world. These include prophecies about Jesus that were fulfilled centuries later in his life, death and resurrection.

4. Does God experience changing emotions and journey through time with us?

The Bible seems to show a God who journeys alongside us and is ceaselessly responsive to all that happens. The central reality about God's nature is summed up in John's words, that "God is love."[9] The emotions attributed to God throughout the Bible arise from and are responses based on that central reality of love. As Psalm 30 tells us, "his anger lasts for a moment, but his favour lasts a life-time."[10]

In what sense can God experience all those emotions that characterize his responses to people in the Bible? If God is timeless and unchanging, nothing can be a surprise, and everything is already fully known by him. There is no temporal succession of moments in time with God. Yet we are told God feels delight when people are faithful to him, and disappointment, grief, and anger at the unfaithfulness of the people he loves.[11] When Jesus uses the parables of the lost sheep, the lost coin and the lost son, he illustrates God's pain at loss, and the "joy in heaven" when the lost is found.[12]

Are these simply poetic, anthropomorphic representations of what God would feel if he wasn't timeless, because timelessness means there is no temporal sequence with God's emotions? We need to emphasize again that we are not talking about the attributes of God, one of which is being

9. 1 John 4:8
10. Ps 30:5
11. e.g. Ps 18:19, 70:4, Prov 3:12, Zeph 3:17
12. Luke 15:7

outside of time. We exist in a temporal world and our human language will always place limitations on talking about this aspect of God. Our attempts to philosophize about God and time are always in danger of falling into incoherence. What makes the ideas of open theology not just coherent, but also very helpful, is that openness relates specifically to how God, in his love and grace, goes about relating to us, given that the act of creation (a temporal act) brought time into existence.

The picture throughout the Bible is how God responds to and interacts with us and with events from moment to moment. God says to Abraham on Mount Moriah when he sees Abraham's obedience, "now I know that you fear God."[13] In response to Moses's prayer, God says, "I'm not going to do what I have planned." God tells Jeremiah, "I may change my mind,"[14] and later "it never came into my mind that they would do this."[15] To Ezekiel, God expresses his hope that "they are very rebellious, but it may be that they will pay attention."[16] He tells Hosea that his anger has now ceased."[17]

The biblical picture is a God who enjoys relationships. The great truth is that God is a Trinity, a dynamic community of Father, Son and Spirit, interrelated in perfect love, perfect oneness. The incarnation shows a God who can become temporal and live among us. As Karl Barth writes, "without God's complete temporality, the content of the Christian message has no shape."[18]

Most of us quite properly live from day to day assuming that the future is genuinely open. We bring our petitionary prayers to God, believing that the future is not already settled. We pray, believing God is genuinely involved in what will happen in the world rather than simply looking on at what he already knows. We are thankful that Jesus still "stands at the door and knocks" and persists in seeking entry into people's lives.[19] We seek guidance from God but guidance is problematic if the outcome of what we will decide to do is already known.

To sum up the biblical evidence, there are plenty of examples where God is presented as open to intercessory persuasion to change his intentions,

13. Gen 22:12
14. Jer 26:3
15. Jer 32:35
16. Ezek 12:3
17. Hos 14:4
18. Barth, *Church Dogmatics,* II. 1, 620
19. Rev 3:20

and that openness is even presented as an attribute of God. "My heart re-coils within me; my compassion grows warm and tender. I will not execute my fierce anger," God tells Hosea.[20] Jonah claims to know that God is "a gracious and compassionate God, slow to anger and abounding in love, a God who relents from sending calamity."[21] There are times when God is said to be disappointed and regretful about what has happened, there are examples of God expressing surprise, and there are times when God is said to be waiting to see how things turn out.

You might say these are just rhetorical ways of intensifying the impact of the words on the reader and not literally true, but that doesn't explain the underlying assumptions of the biblical writers throughout the whole Bible that God longs to be with us on our journey of change, and God can be genuinely influenced by our prayers and by our faithfulness to the Holy Spirit's leading. The future is never fixed or closed, and God is waiting with the desire that our lives should reflect his love and goodness, and enable his will to be done on earth as in heaven. The whole Bible speaks of the intensity of God's love for the whole world, and his grief when we turn away and follow destructive paths.

Jesus's prayer in John's gospel follows a similar pattern. He is thankful for what his Father has done and is doing now, and hoping that in the future his followers will be unified in their lives and in their faithfulness to him, so that people will turn to God and become followers of Christ.[22] Alongside this open future are God's promised, guaranteed outcomes, most notably God's new creation when Jesus returns to complete his kingdom.

It seems clear that the freedom given to humanity and to the universe itself is part of God's purpose, and that leaves the future genuinely open and not predetermined or foreordained by God. Canon Bill Vanstone puts it well when he claims that the creation's security lies not in some prede-termined plan, but in God's "unsparing love that will not abandon a single fragment of it."[23]

---

20. Hos 11:8–9
21. Jon 4:2
22. John 17:1–26
23. Vanstone, *Love's Endeavour*

5. Is the future known to God in his relationship with the creation?

The writers of *The Openness of God*, wanted to show that the biblical picture is that God has respected the freedom given to his creation. This means that God has voluntarily limited his foreknowledge, and experiences time in a way that is similar to how we experience it, and so the future is open and unknowable. God allows us to take part in bringing the future into being, meaning that "God's knowledge of the world is dynamic rather than static."[24]

William Lane Craig, in his book, *Time and Eternity: Exploring God's Relationship to Time,* develops this open view of God's relationship with his creation. He explains that in the act of creation, God has shown respect for his gift of freedom by allowing a future that is genuinely open and unknowable not just to us but also to God himself. Clark Pinnock in *The Openness of God* sees God's foreknowledge "voluntarily self-limited, making room for creaturely freedom" as an act of his "creative goodness"[25]

All of this in no way challenges or denies God's omniscience. It would be perfectly possible for God to have foreknowledge of everything that was going to happen, but the message of the Bible and our own experience of God lead to the conclusion that God has voluntarily limited his foreknowledge to make the freedom of life in his creation meaningful. Willian Lane Craig sums it up neatly: "God without creation is timeless; God with creation is temporal."[26]

On the one hand, God is eternal and outside of time and space, but at the same time he journeys with us and relates to us in all our time-bound experiences. Greg Boyd in his book, *God of the Possible: A Biblical Introduction to the Open View of God*, agrees that a genuinely open future doesn't put a limit on God's omniscience. It's not a question of God's perfect knowledge of reality. It's a question of whether there is a section of reality that God has chosen to remain genuinely open. Just as we live in a universe in which the past is fixed and we can't go back and redo it, so too the future is open and there is nothing yet to know, apart from those things that are parts of God's revealed plan.

---

24. Pinnock, *The Openness of God,* Preface
25. Pinnock, *The Openness of God*
26. Craig, *Time and Eternity*

The belief that time in our universe moves from a fixed past to an open future is summed up in Arthur Peacocke's memorable description of God as the "improvisor of unsurpassed ingenuity."[27] This is why we can have complete confidence that the love, goodness and power of God will always oversee his gift of freedom, and that God is constantly involved, always active and at work in our lives and our world.

6. But isn't God infinite in wisdom?

While there is good biblical evidence that God only knows events as they happen, we need to recognize that the wisdom and understanding of God are infinite. While God journeys through life with us, the ultimate reassurance is clearly expressed in both Old and New Testaments. "Great is our Lord and of great power. His understanding is infinite," says the Psalmist.[28] "O the depth of the riches of the wisdom and knowledge of God. How unsearchable are his judgments and his ways past finding out," writes Paul.[29]

Do infinite wisdom and understanding mean we're just playing with words when we say that God has voluntarily limited his knowledge of the future? First, the future is genuinely open, because God in his wisdom can foresee what may well happen, but not know the unknowable. God's wisdom doesn't negate the freedom given to us and to the created universe. We are responsible for our sinful choices. God isn't actively allowing sin and evil to happen.

Second, God's infinite wisdom allows us to rejoice in God as the "improvisor of unsurpassed ingenuity," in Peacocke's words. God's responses are passionately felt and exercised with infinite understanding, infinite wisdom, and best of all, infinite love for his creation. The gift of freedom means that God is dealing with all that happens, the good and the bad, in real time, and not looking on as a God who has already known it all from before the world began.

27. Peacocke, *Paths from Science*
28. Ps 147:5
29. Rom 11:33

7. So is God in control?

Humanity and the universe itself have been given the respect of freedom to act and evolve so that, as C. S. Lewis explains so well, we can freely and voluntarily choose to be united with him and with others.[30] We are thankful that God is in charge and that his loving purposes for the universe will come about. Can we then say that God is sovereign and in control? Yes, but we need to know what we mean.

If we accept that an open view of God's relationship with the creation is closest to a biblical view, then "God is in control" doesn't mean that God has predetermined all that happens or that he knows our future actions and chooses to allow some things and not others. It means that God in his sovereignty is responding to all that happens in the creation moment by moment, and in his infinite wisdom, can intervene as he chooses. Our cries and prayers are heard and answered as God desires.

Jesus's great commission to us to go and make disciples of all nations is based on one foundation, that Jesus is Lord of all creation. "All authority in heaven and on earth has been given to me," was the outcome of all that was achieved through the death and resurrection of God's Messiah.[31] It is absolutely sure that in the future "every knee shall bow and every tongue acknowledge that Jesus Christ is Lord."[32] Nothing we have discussed about how God relates to his creation challenges the reality of God's sovereignty and Christ's Lordship over everything in heaven and on earth.

At the same time, as N. T. Wright suggests in his book, *God and the Pandemic*, Jesus has redefined for us the practical significance of words like kingdom, sovereignty, control, power, and authority.[33] "Whoever wants to be great among you shall be your servant," for "the son of man did not come to be served, but to serve, and give his life as a ransom for many."[34] "The greatest must be the servant of all,"[35] and our model for life is the way God exercises his power and sovereignty through love and grace.

Possibly the most frequently repeated encouragement in the Bible is "Do not be afraid." The reason is always the same. There is a God who is

---

30. Lewis, *Mere Christianity*, 48

31. Matt 28:18

32. Phil 2:10–11

33. Wright, *God and the Pandemic*, ch.3

34. Matt 20:26–28

35. Matt 23:11

completely committed to the world he has created, a God of love, of wisdom, and of power, and the best evidence for this is his coming into human history in the person of Jesus. Jesus demonstrated that in the freedom we have to choose, act, and learn, God journeys with us, guides and supports us in the person of God's Holy Spirit who accompanies us in all the challenges and opportunities of life, and will never abandon us, even when our mistakes are many. As the biblical proverb says, "the heart of a man plans his way, but the Lord directs his steps."[36]

That is exactly the control over our lives that we need. On top of that, the ultimate future is completely guaranteed. There's a repeated promise in both the Old and New Testaments that there will be "a new heaven and new earth" in the future, when God's creation will be restored and renewed.[37] That's a process that has begun now and is the day-to-day task of all who follow Christ.

8. Does prayer change things?

Prayer is God's most precious gift to us, rather than the duty we sometimes make it out to be. The respect God shows us is as a heavenly parent with whom we can have two-way communication at any and every moment through our lives. A key part of our spiritual health is putting into words our thanks, our worship, our regrets, and our longings to God.

But we all experience times of great distress, of grief, of upset, when putting feelings into words is beyond us, and Paul assures us that "the Spirit helps us in our weakness. We do not know what we ought to pray for, but the Spirit intercedes for us with groanings too deep for words."[38] Knowing God's Spirit carries the burden of bringing our thoughts and feelings to God is a gift of grace. At the same time, we can aim for what St Basil the Great, 4th century Bishop of Caesarea, set before us as a goal. "Pray without ceasing: if you pray not only in words, but unite yourself to God through all the course of life, so your life is made one ceaseless and uninterrupted prayer."[39]

The picture the Bible gives us of petitionary prayer is a genuinely instrumental one, making new possibilities come about. We are called to live

---

36. Prov 16:9
37. Isa 65:17 & 66:22, 2 Pet 3:13, Rev 21:1–5
38. Rom 8:26
39. St Basil the Great. "On Giving Thanks"

in partnership with God in his interaction with the world, and it may be that there are outcomes that can only come about if we bring them to God in our prayers.

In his book, *Knocking on Heaven's Door*, David Crump does a fine job presenting us with a theology of prayer. He claims that faith is not so much a matter of degree, but rather a simple condition that we believe God hears and answers. He also makes clear that Jesus's prayer in Gethsemane is our great model. It was encircled with faith ("Father, everything is possible for you"), but also with total affirmation of God's loving wisdom ("yet not what I will, but what you will").[40] Jesus models how prayer actively aligns us with God, especially when it is based on what we learn from Christ's self-sacrifice on the cross, rather than for personal gain.

Henri Nouwen has written a helpful call to prayer called *Reaching Out*, because prayer is reaching out to God and entering a world beyond the narrow boundaries of our own minds. Prayer, therefore, is a comfort as well as adventure because God is greater than all we can think or imagine. We bring our own and other people's struggles to God, praying for deliverance, knowing that prayer for help will always be answered, for God can be trusted to be with us. If the answer is not a change in our physical circumstances, it will certainly be to come alongside us and give strength through all the challenges of life.

Further Discussion

1. How do you understand Jesus's words in his great commission. when he said "all authority in heaven and on earth has been given to me" (Matthew 28:18)?

2. Do you think it's possible that God has limited his foreknowledge of the future, and journeys through our lives with us as we experience time and change, so that the future remains genuinely open?

40. Mark 14:36

Chapter 9

Focus on Christian Mission

1. What is the goal of Christian mission?

2. How does Christian mission relate to a postmodern world?

3. How do we keep mission as our first priority?

4. What can we learn about mission from Matthew's gospel?

5. What does Christian mission have to say about climate change?

1. What is the goal of Christian mission?

In *A Generous Orthodoxy*, Brian McLaren seeks an inclusive definition of Christian mission. His suggestion is "to be and make disciples of Jesus Christ in authentic community for the good of the world."[1] McLaren claims Christians too often see their own redemption as the primary goal, followed by commitment to the church, with the world an afterthought in our thoughts and actions. This should be reversed, with our impact on those outside the church being our first concern.

In his book, *The Great Story and the Great Commission*, Chris Wright takes the "five marks of mission" agreed by the Anglican Consultative Council in 1984, and shows how they connect beautifully with Jesus's Great Commission.[2] Jesus's commission is recorded in Matthew 28:18–20. "All authority in heaven and on earth has been given to me. Therefore, go and

---

1. McLaren, *A Generous Orthodoxy*
2. Wright, *The Great Story*, 60–74

make disciples of all nations, baptizing them in the name of the Father and of the Son and of the Holy Spirit, and teaching them to obey everything I have commanded you. And surely I am with you always, to the very end of the age."

The Anglican Communion's five marks of mission, as Wright summarises them, are evangelism (proclaiming the good news), teaching (nurturing believers and building the church), compassion (responding to needs), justice (transforming social structures), and care for creation. The goal of mission remains clear, for all five of the "marks" are already embedded in Jesus's great commission, in the Lordship of Jesus over both heaven and the earth, in making disciples who follow his example, and in obeying all the teaching that he has left us.

Seeing evangelism and social action as unrelated is clearly rejected. Love for the world involves both, and discipleship always seeks to reach out and bring blessing, shalom, to all whether they respond to the gospel or not. Having insisted that mission unites demonstration of the gospel in loving service with the proclamation of the good news of Jesus, his life, death and resurrection, McLaren makes the important claim that we also need a clear "theology of connection, collaboration and partnership." Partnering with other community organizations not only means wiser use of our limited resources, but also increases our impact on the communities we live in.

N. T. Wright in *Surprised by Hope* emphasizes how building God's kingdom in the world is our calling that will last into God's new world when Christ returns. Building a better world for the poor, the oppressed, the abused, the hungry, is not an extra to the gospel. Our mission is to bring God's rule into the world here and now until it is completed in God's future.[3] In all of this, integrated mission means we are called to be disciples of Jesus both in community and as individuals, in who we are, what we do, and what we say.

2. How does Christian mission relate to a postmodern world?

We live in a world dominated by two approaches to truth, with authoritarianism at one extreme and postmodernism at the other. We need to show that there is a different, liberating approach to truth found in the overarching biblical story that leads us from the creation of the universe through to

---

3. Wright, *Surprised by Hope*

the renewal of all things in God's new earth, with Jesus as the foundation and connecting thread.

The key feature of postmodernism is rejection of all universal systems and ideas that claim objective truth. Postmodernism dismisses any system that sees the world in terms of a single story (a metanarrative) that claims universal relevance and application. French philosopher Jean-François Lyotard defined postmodernism as "incredulity toward metanarratives."[4] All overarching narratives are suspect because they usually have hidden, oppressive purposes or outcomes.

Experience shows that one dominating point of view is usually more concerned with increasing power rather than a search for truth. We've seen many dominating systems throughout history. Examples such as ancient Rome and other more modern forms of imperialism, such as Fascism, Naziism, Communism, and many types of religious fundamentalism, share an insistence that there is one way of being and doing, and so become authoritarian and dangerous.

The biblical story is a genuine metanarrative without the dangers that postmodernism fears and authoritarianism represents. First, it's a story told through a vast diversity of contexts. Diversity is celebrated, because it's about a God who has always spoken and acted in a multitude of ways to different people in different contexts.

Second, the biblical story has no enforcement, because it's a universalism of love shown in the life, death and resurrection of Jesus, with the goal of a new earth of love and goodness, begun now and completed when Jesus returns. Christian proclamation sees human freedom as a God-given gift, and as Richard Baulkham writes "it is the very nature of Christian truth that it cannot be coerced."[5] This sets apart the Christian "grand story" as a thoroughly liberating story of love and hope.

There's a beautiful event described in Luke's gospel. Just after Jesus was crucified, a couple, Cleopas and Mary, are on their way home from Jerusalem, devastated because the hope they had of Jesus bringing liberation for their nation has been extinguished.[6]

A stranger joins them on their journey and asks why they're so dejected. They explain that "we hoped Jesus was the one who was going to

---

4. Lyotard, *The Postmodern Condition*

5. Baulkham, *Bible and Mission*

6. Luke 24:13–35. Some scholars believe that Cleopas and his companion may be the Clopas and his wife, Mary, mentioned in John 19:25

redeem Israel." The stranger listens to all they say and then tells them they need to understand the story in a completely new way. "And beginning with Moses and all the prophets, he explained what was said in all the Scriptures concerning himself."

When they reach their home, they invite the stranger in for a meal and it's not until he "took bread, gave thanks, broke it and began to give it to them," that they realize this is Jesus, the one they hoped would set them free, but who was crucified and buried several days before.

Despair turns to hope and joy and they set off back to Jerusalem to spread the good news that Jesus is alive, risen from the dead, and to join the task of building what the resurrection of Jesus has begun: a transformed world, God's kingdom, where his will is done on earth, as it is in heaven.

If Christianity is a metanarrative, it's possibly unique because it's a story governed by love and hope, and it doesn't exercise or want power over how people live. It celebrates diversity, and if it uses the word "command," then it's in the context of Jesus's words, "a new commandment I give to you, that you love one another."[7]

3. How do we keep mission as our first priority?

It was a joy to see some great examples of effective church mission during our time working in Indonesia. At its best, in a context of serious social deprivation, local churches reached out in self-sacrificial ways that put into practice the prophetic calling in the Bible to combat social problems of poverty and inequality, and at the same time provide the assurance that Paul gave the people in first century Rome, that not "trouble or hardship or persecution or famine or nakedness or danger or sword . . . and neither death nor life, neither angels nor demons, neither the present nor the future, nor any powers, neither height nor depth, nor anything else in all creation, will be able to separate us from the love of God that is in Christ Jesus our Lord."[8]

The central message of the prophets was that the proper context for worship that God accepts is social justice, care for the poor and the marginalized, ending inequality, exploitation and oppression.[9] James begins his New Testament letter with the same message to the early churches. True

---

7. John 13:34

8. Rom 8:35–39

9. Isa 1:17, Jer 5:27–28, Amos 2:6–7, Mic 6:6–8, Mal 3:5

religion is to care for the poor and the marginalized.[10] Jesus was clear that his mission was to fulfil the same prophetic message, quoting Isaiah. "The Spirit of the Lord is upon me, because he has anointed me to proclaim good news to the poor. He has sent me to proclaim freedom for the prisoners, recovery of sight for the blind, and to set the oppressed free."[11]

Richard Foster, in his book, *Celebration of Discipline*, sums up the importance of integrating spiritual disciplines with our task of changing the world for the better. Spiritual disciplines "are not a set of pious exercises for the devout."[12] They are a call to work for peace, justice and equality.

4. What can we learn about mission from Matthew's gospel?

The beatitudes, a series of sayings of Jesus recorded in Matthew and Luke, tell us about groups of people who are specially blessed in the kingdom of God. As Dallas Willard emphasizes in *The Divine Conspiracy*, they show that those who have no hope in life, those who think they have nothing to offer, those whom society considers losers or outsiders, are the very people who will discover God is on their side and that they are blessed in the kingdom of God. In this sense, the beatitudes "are pronouncements of grace,"[13] for Jesus came to change the world and put things right. The way we demonstrate and proclaim the good news of the kingdom of God is by living out these messages of blessing, showing as well as telling people everywhere that there is hope for them, whatever their circumstances.

At the outset of his work, Jesus demonstrated the programme he had announced by spending his time with the poor, the rejected, the outsiders, the victimized, those on the margins of society, and showed a special concern for the sick and disabled, the lepers, the mentally ill, the sex workers, the foreigners, the "sinners" whom society looked down on. When Jesus talked about his disciples being the salt of the earth and the light of the world, he is calling us to be the salt that changes the way things are done in the world, and the light that points to the God whose love and power are the source of all life.

Matthew is showing us the coming of a radically new kingdom in the person of Jesus. First, he tells us about his genealogy, the "genesis" of Jesus

10. Isa 1:17, Jer 5:27–28, Amos 2:6–7, Mic 6:6–8, Mal 3:5
11. Luke 4:18–21 & Isa 61:1–3
12. Foster, *Celebration of Discipline* 1–12
13. Willard, *The Divine Conspiracy*

Christ in Matthew 1:1. He uses the word 'genesis' again in Matthew 19:28 for the "regeneration" of all things which Jesus will bring about when he returns at the end of time to set up his kingdom in all its fullness.

Matthew's genealogy sets out Matthew's radical approach at the very beginning of his gospel. Jewish genealogies usually only mention male ancestors. Matthew is determined to select key ancestors that show what kind of new kingdom Jesus has brought. Ignoring the normal tradition of the line of only male ancestors, we hear of female foreigners (Rahab a Canaanite, Ruth a Moabite), Tamar, (maybe also a Canaanite but this is disputed), whose complex liaison with her father-in-law Judah made her an ancestor of Jesus through her and Judah's son, Perez, and a motley crew of the good and the bad, leading to the beautiful choice of a very ordinary young girl, Mary. And why is Uriah included in a genealogy of Jesus? He had no part in Jesus's ancestry. David begat Solomon by Bathsheba who had been the wife of Uriah. Uriah was an innocent victim of great injustice, killed by king David so that he could obtain Bathsheba.

It's clear from the outset of Matthew's gospel that the mission of Jesus's kingdom will involve caring for foreigners and immigrants, standing up for the rights of women, fighting injustice of all kinds, defending those who are victims of our economic system, and opposing those in power who fail to defend the poor and the weak, and who take away the lifeline of protection for those in need.

In Matthew's gospel, it's the powerful, like Herod, who want to destroy Jesus. It's the wise, who in this case come from Persia, or perhaps Babylon, who recognize Jesus. And it's to Egypt that Jesus goes to escape being killed. If Matthew chapter 1 is the start of a new book of Genesis, then Matthew chapter 2 is a new story of Exodus, except this time Jesus is safe in Egypt until Herod's death.

Before we come to Jesus's Great Commission to go into all the world with the good news of the gospel,[14] Matthew shows that Jesus's mission reinforces the Old Testament prophets' message of God's love for and affirmation of all nations in the world. God's mission hates sectarianism and racism of all kinds. Sectarianism puts down and demonizes one section of a community or one group of people. The mission of God will always be one of love and inclusive welcome to all people.

Matthew shows that the salt of God's kingdom is at work among the poor, the sick, the disabled, the marginalised, the rejected, the children, the

14. Matt 28:19

oppressed. Then the light points to the reason for all this good work, the love of God and the forgiveness that has come to human beings through Jesus's death, and the new kingdom brought into being through his resurrection. The blessings on groups of people in the beatitudes in Matthew 5 assure all who think they have nothing to offer that they are especially welcome in God's kingdom, and also call on us to adopt characteristics that don't go with worldly success: mourning the injustice in the world, peacemaking, purity of heart, hunger and thirst for God's righteousness.

5. What does Christian mission have to say about climate change?

Maybe the best-known statement in the Bible is in John's gospel: "God so loves the world that he gave his only son."[15] We have a great tendency to read statements like that in a purely anthropocentric way, as if it is humanity alone that is the focus of God's love. The message of the Bible is much wider. God loves and calls us to cherish and protect the whole earth. God gave his only son so that we "should not perish." The same warning to avoid people "perishing" has been used at recent Climate Change Conferences.

The World Council of Churches declared in 2013: "Creation has been misused and we face threats to the balance of life, a growing ecological crisis and the effects of climate change. These are signs of our disordered relations with God, with one another and with creation, and we confess that they dishonour God's gift of life."[16] David Atkinson wrote in 2015 that "underneath the lack of urgency among Christians is a belief that environmental concern, caring for the creation, is not really a Christian priority." It is just "a worthy thing to do if you have time.[17] Has that lack of urgency changed?

On the 50th anniversary of Earth Day in 2020, Johan Rockström, director of the Potsdam Institute for Climate Impact Research was joined by Swedish activist, Greta Thunberg, to call on the world to heed the lessons of the Covid 19 pandemic when applied to the dangers of climate change. They warned that the key lesson from the pandemic is the need for governments to pay more heed to scientific warnings: "If the coronavirus crisis has shown us one thing, it is that our society is not sustainable. If one

15. John 3:16
16. *The Ecumenical Review*, "God's Gift"
17. Atkinson, "Why we in the churches"

single virus can destroy economies in a couple of weeks, it shows we are not thinking long-term and taking risks into account. We have underestimated the shocks. We need to build more shock absorbers into the system. It's not worth taking the risk."[18]

Christian Aid speaks for all who want to see Christians and churches taking responsibility for our God-given job of caring for the earth. They warn that "right now, millions of the world's poorest people are feeling the worst impacts of climate change, and experts predict more floods, drought and extreme weather patterns to come. For those living in poverty, this means more hunger, conflict and insecurity, and a more uncertain future for us all." Christian charities like Christian Aid, Tearfund and CAFOD (Catholic Agency for Overseas Development) have led the way in mobilizing young and old to press for urgent action.

We know some of the things we can do as individuals and households: reduce, reuse and recycle, avoid plastic, walk or bike more, use public transport, use an electric car, decrease air travel, cut food waste, eat less meat, buy locally grown food, turn off lights, unplug electrical devices, reduce consumption of water, use renewable energy and energy-efficient products, cut down on the use of paper.

Churches have the role of pressing governments to act on issues like the ones below that Friends of the Earth call us to focus on, asking us to vote for those who will work towards:

- using public transport, electric cars at affordable prices, and cutting down frequent flying.
- using renewable clean energy from the wind, sun and sea.
- having well insulated homes, heated mainly by electricity.
- nature-friendly farming, low meat and dairy diets and doubling the size of our forests.
- a stop to wasting food and using single-use plastics and short-lived products that end up in landfill.
- international justice for poorer countries who suffer the most from climate change, but have contributed the least to global carbon emissions. We need to say we will play a significant part in supporting vulnerable countries.[19]

18. Rockstrom, "Earth Day"
19. Friends of the Earth, "Coronavirus"

Further Discussion

1. Are the Lambeth Conference's five marks of mission, (proclamation, teaching and nurturing, meeting people's needs, transforming unjust social structures and caring for the creation) equally important?

2. Are McLaren's words, "a transformation plan for the earth" a good description of Christian mission?

3. Should dealing with climate change be a high priority for Christian mission?

Chapter 10

Some Contemporary Issues

1. How should our churches show welcome, respect, and love for the lesbian, gay, and transgender community?

2. Do the teaching and example of Jesus mean we ought to be pacifists?

3. What should our attitude be to other religions?

4. Could AI mean the end of humanity as we know it?

5. What should characterize a Christian approach to immigration?

1. How should our churches show welcome, respect and love for the lesbian, gay, and transgender community?

(i) On a journey

An attempt to give a biblical answer to this question is vitally important. First, LGBTQ people[1] who are not Christians treat with scorn a Christianity with nothing but cold condemnation to offer them. Second, many Christians who are part of the LGBTQ community find themselves rejected and even excluded by many of our churches. If God's love for us isn't the first thing people hear and experience, then the famous words of John 3:16, that "God so loved the world that he gave his son," lose their meaning.

The great American theologian, Walter Brueggemann, author of more than 150 scholarly studies on the Bible, wrote a recent online piece called

---

1. Lesbian, Gay, Bisexual, Transgender, Questioning

"The Book of Amos shows how God's emancipatory embrace includes LG-BTQ people." He describes how the Old Testament prophets kept calling attention to the global inclusiveness of Yahweh's love and care.

The prophet Amos, writing in the 8th century BC, warns Israel that they are not uniquely favoured by God. He writes, "Are not you Israelites the same to me as the Cushites?" declares the Lord. "Did I not bring Israel up from Egypt, the Philistines from Caphtor and the Arameans from Kir?"[2] The exodus from Egypt was a wonderful divine intervention in Israel's history, but Amos reminds them that other peoples, seen as Israel's enemies, experienced their own God-given exoduses.

Brueggemann points out that the same process of learning about the global extent of God's love and goodness is the Christian church's history too. Just as the Jewish people had to learn that God's love and goodness weren't just specially focused on them, so the early Christian Jews had to learn that in Christ there was "neither Jew nor Gentile, neither slave nor free, neither male nor female."[3]

Brueggemann sees the same process in the growth of the church. We had to learn that there was no superior role for white Europeans in interpreting God's word and being God's people. We've had to learn that men are not favoured over women in power or authority in the church. We're now in the process of learning that heterosexual people are not loved and favoured by God over LGBTQ people. There are no boundaries of nationality, race, sexuality or gender, for God will never be constrained by our boxes and boundaries.

(ii) Starting points

We need to look at the importance of the LGBTQ community in the life of the church in the context of the Bible, and I do this willingly, because I share a belief in the Bible as God's word to us and a guide through issues we meet in life.

Jesus has given us as his followers one task, to bring the good news of God's love and salvation to every person in every nation in the world, because, as John tells us in his gospel, "God did not send his Son into the world to condemn the world, but to save the world through him."[4] There's

2. Amos 9:7

3. Gal 3:28

4. John 3:17

a huge worldwide community of LGBTQ people who need to be shown God's love for them, and a community of Christian LGBTQ people with whom we're partners in the work of the gospel. If what we have to say is just condemnation, then we're denying our mission.

The most important starting point is to say that values and moral principles like love, commitment, monogamy, and rejection of promiscuity apply to all of us and to all good relationships, no matter what our natural identity is. A Christian, and indeed a human perspective, ought to see heterosexual and same-sex relationships subject to the same moral principles and values.

(iii) A note about language

The language we use can be a reconciler, or it can be a weapon to reinforce attitudes that cause rejection and exclusion. Being challenged about the language we use can help our thinking about a topic. The word "homosexual" is regarded as unhelpful nowadays because it suggests an identity based simply on sexual orientation rather than on broader human characteristics. Sexual orientation is just one aspect of those human characteristics. Gay on its own tends to be male oriented, so it's better to refer to gay and lesbian. In order to include transgender people and people questioning their identity, we use the term LGBTQ people.

As the World Health Organization (WHO) makes clear, sex is based on biological and physiological characteristics that are generally assigned at birth, hence the term natal sex. Gender is largely a social construct, with learned characteristics, attributes, roles, and behaviours, and is a broad spectrum. A person's gender may or may not correspond with their sex. A person whose gender identity is different from their natal sex might identify as transgender.[5]

(iv) Centuries of persecution

One of the most persecuted groups in world history has been people from the LGBTQ community. Hostility, discrimination and exclusion have been part of a continuum leading to criminalization and persecution worldwide, and there's a deep irony if those who strongly condemn global persecution

5. WHO, "Gender"

of Christians and other religious groups are at the forefront of condemning and excluding gay and lesbian people. One of the saddest aspects is that religious views have contributed to what gay and lesbian people have suffered, and some of those attitudes claim to be based on the Bible.

(v) Natural identity

There are only three specific references in the New Testament to same sex relationships[6] and there was little scientific understanding of identity and orientation available to New Testament writers. There has been plenty of modern research into the links between biology and orientation and it still remains a complex question, but it seems clear that genetic and hormonal factors play the main role in determining natural identity and sexual orientation. Choice and environmental and cultural factors may play a part, but in many parts of the world it takes extreme courage to come out as gay or lesbian, and it seems clear that biological factors are dominant. Certainly, orientation is much broader than just sexual desire.

(vi) The apostle Paul's views

There are at least four aspects to what is involved in biblical interpretation.[7] We need to understand as much as possible about the historical and the cultural context of the text we're reading. Also, as C. S. Lewis reminds us, we need to read it in its literary, genre-specific context.[8] Bearing in mind those three contexts, we then need to examine the text itself in detail. Then we may be ready to apply it to ourselves and our lives today.

You might expect me to begin with what Jesus said, rather than with Paul, but Jesus isn't recorded saying anything directly about same-sex relationships. What we do see in Jesus is warm-hearted love for people of all kinds, alongside mixing, eating and drinking with those marginalized in any way, and his criticism is usually reserved for those religious people who think they are holier than others. There's a suggestion that Jesus's extreme

6. Rom 1:18–2:2; 1 Cor 6:9–10, 1 Tim 1:8–10
7. Zowada, "What is Biblical Hermeneutics?"
8. Lewis, "Fern-seed"

anger about making a child to "stumble," (Greek, *skandalizo*),[9] might refer to sexual abuse of children.

In reading Paul's three references to same-sex relationships, it's essential to see the larger context. There are many summaries available, and a detailed and comprehensive one that I recommend is "Same-sex relationships: A 1st-century perspective," by Professor of New Testament at Murdoch University in Australia, William Loader.

Paul grew up as a Jew, zealous to protect Judaism from Hellenistic influences. Antioch, close to Tarsus where Paul was born, was a center of Hellenistic Judaism, bringing liberal influences that Paul fought against. Greek influences also permeated the culture of the Roman Empire where Paul lived and worked. Educated Romans learnt Greek, and Greek philosophy, religion, culture, and science blended with Roman culture. Paul himself spoke and wrote his letters to the churches in *Koine* ("common") Greek, the dialect that unified speakers of Greek across the Roman Empire.

There was no word for "homosexual" in Greek or Latin in Paul's time, just as there was no concept of homosexuality as we know it today, in the Old Testament. The Old Testament Torah speaks only of certain sexual acts forbidden to Jews, often in the context of incestuous actions, in the codes of clean and unclean actions. Paul had to coin or borrow a word unknown in other ancient writings to describe the type of sexual activity he refers to in 1 Corinthians 6: 9–10 and 1 Timothy 1: 8–10.

The background to Paul's three references is a Greek and Roman culture where commercial, coercive, exploitative, and abusive practices were common, and that was certainly true of Roman idolatry and shrine prostitution, and the promiscuous and orgiastic practices associated with it. Pederasty was the Greek practice of elite older men adopting young men or boys for sexual purposes, to some extent mirroring the marriage context of older men taking young women or girls. Slaves and non-citizens of Rome were especially vulnerable to being used for sexual practices.

Eugene Peterson, theologian and writer of *The Message: The Bible in Contemporary Language*, points out that "the biblical world had no notion of what is being proposed now, same-sex couples committed by marriage covenant to faithfulness."[10] Biblical condemnation is focused on a range of practices that would also be offensive in heterosexual relationships. No

---

9. Matt 18: 5–6 and Mark 9:42

10. Collier, *A Burning in My Bones*

doubt there were same-sex relationships in Paul's time that were loving and committed, but they would never be seen as a moral ideal.

Another aspect of context is to remember that Paul didn't write his letters in chapters. Our modern chapter divisions are arbitrary. It's easy to read Paul's list of practices that he says anger God in Romans chapter 1, and then ignore Paul's point about them in the second chapter. Paul lists the practices in chapter 1 and follows that with the statement that begins chapter 2: "You, therefore, have no excuse, you who pass judgment on someone else," because we're all in the same position before God. Those who use Romans 1 to condemn, take note.

That still leaves the question of the actual sin identified in Romans 1. It's called "shameful acts, inflamed with lust."[11] In a context of commercial, exploitative and abusive same-sex practices, it's no surprise if Paul spoke out vehemently against acceptance of what often amounted to abuse of other people, including children and young people. We have to decide whether we believe Paul's description is the same thing as loving actions within committed, monogamous same-sex relationships.

It's also worth noting that he had to coin or borrow a word unknown in other ancient writings to describe the type of sexual activity he refers to in 1 Corinthians 6: 9–10 and 1 Timothy 1: 8–10. Greek had no special word for homosexuality, presumably because it saw no need to regard homosexuality and heterosexuality as separate identities. It's been suggested that the only words available to Paul at the time referred to prostitution between men and women, and Paul needed a word specifying prostitution involving two men.[12]

(vii) The need for a companion

The Bible tells us in Genesis that it's not good for a man to be alone, and that God has provided the norm of a companion, a partner.[13] Paul found being single good because it freed him to concentrate on his mission, but had no problem praising marriage too, because it was "better to marry than to burn with passion."[14] Are gay and lesbian people excluded from this? Christians put great emphasis on loving, committed, monogamous relationships

11. Rom 1:27
12. Wright, "Homosexuals or Prostitutes?"
13. Gen 2:18
14. 1 Cor 7:9

as the context for expressing their sexual identity, but often don't allow the same context to people whose identity is gay or lesbian.

(viii) Biblical norms

Those who oppose same-sex relationships often point out that the biblical norm is the partnership of a man and a woman.[15] However, it's obvious that heterosexual relationships will be the norm, as one of the main purposes is to "be fruitful and multiply."[16] But a norm doesn't mean that there's something wrong with everyone for whom the norm isn't possible. It should never leave those in different relationships, (including those who marry but aren't able to have children), feeling second-rate.

(ix) Applying the Bible to our social context

In his authorized biography, where Eugene Peterson is recorded as saying that there is no concept of "same-sex couples committed by marriage covenant to faithfulness," he goes on to point out that in reading the Bible, it's essential to put what we read into its historical context. He uses the commonness of polygamy in the Hebrew world, and King David's nine wives, as an example of how we read with awareness that "matters of sexuality are very much shaped by culture."[17]

Peterson was saying that it's our job to apply general biblical principles to the social cultures of the world we live in. We need to adapt what we find in the Bible about women in leadership, about slavery in society, and about marriage relationships to the very different world of our time.

Let me give another example of reading the Bible and the need to apply it to our present social and cultural context. Paul tells the Corinthian church that men should not cover their heads in church, but women should cover their heads, because the man is "the image and glory of God, and the woman is the glory of man."[18] Later, in the same chapter, Paul uses the de-

---

15. Gen 2:24

16. Gen 1:28

17. Just before his death in 2018, it seems Peterson went on to deny support for same-sex marriages, but that doesn't remove the validity of his earlier opinions recorded in Collier's biography of him.

18. 1 Cor 11:3–6

scriptions *para physis* meaning "unnatural," and *atimia* meaning "disgraceful," to describe men having long hair.[19]

Are we supposed to apply today what Paul is telling us about how disgraceful and unnatural it is for men to grow their hair long, and important for women to show their secondary position with regard to men being the image and glory of God, by keeping their hair covered in church? Much has been written on the meaning of Paul's use of *para physis* (against nature), ranging from "unconventional" to "biologically abnormal" to "diverging from what God has ordained." You might ask why so much fuss about men having long hair (which, if nature has its way, grows long anyway). Today we have a different understanding of the relationship between men and women, the position of women in society, the need for a man to have just one wife, and the rightness or wrongness of slavery in society. Cultural context is a wonderful thing!

(x) Love and dignity

The Bible constantly affirms human dignity. Life is a sacred gift of God and humans are in his image. "And these three remain," writes Paul, "faith, hope and love. But the greatest of these is love."[20] "God is love," writes John.[21] Are people who read their Bibles really saying that gay and lesbian people should be left to struggle with being alone, rejected and lacking self-worth because of their natural identity?

(xi) Understanding gender

With the growing number of people identifying as transgender, where their gender identity or gender expression is different from their natal sex, we need to recognize the challenges presented by this as well as providing helpful support. It's a complex issue and needs more exploration that these short paragraphs can give it. The World Health Organization explains that gender is largely a social construct, it is fluid, and it's a very broad spectrum.

19. 1 Cor 11:14

20. 1 Cor 13:13

21. 1 John 4:7

Gender issues become especially challenging when someone feels "a mismatch between their anatomical sex and their gender identity."[22]

Our starting point again is clear. "God so loved this world that he gave his only son,"[23] and the world God loves is one of extraordinary variety and diversity. Our task is to share God's love with the whole world, and for the Bible to be used as a weapon to reinforce rejection and exclusion of people is the opposite of the mission of Jesus. Many of us were brought up in a culture of condemnation of gay and lesbian people, and we've been through the process of growth that Brueggemann described earlier, into what we hope is greater understanding. Maybe we can learn from our experience and also develop a more truly Christian approach to issues of gender.

For many of us, our gender identity is very much governed by traditional, social expectations of appearance, behaviour, roles and language, and we've never had to question our gender identity. It would be wonderful if there were no stereotypes and traditional expectations for people, whatever their natal sex. There are cultural differences globally, but probably no society in which conformity to expectations doesn't apply. People who find that their natural identity doesn't fit with the sex they were born with endure stigma, rejection, discrimination, bullying, hate crimes and sometimes assault in response to their expression of what they know as their true gender identity.

The situation for children increasingly becoming aware of the issue of transgender, often while still at primary school, is a challenge. The UK National Health Service (NHS) advice rightly tells us that wise support is needed through childhood and into puberty because some children will come to see it as a transitional stage that they pass through on their journey. If gender is fluid and changeable, then it seems vital to safeguard children from long-term decisions before they are old enough to be sure.

(xii) Celebrating diversity

There are some obvious things we can do. For those who are working out the relationship between their gender and their natal sex, we can provide positive support where all are equally loved and respected. We can do everything possible to remove shame or guilt. We are all on a spectrum with regard to how we express our gender, and no-one should be made to feel

22. World Health Organization, "Gender and Health"
23. John 3:16

uncomfortable about how they dress, how they look and how they are addressed. If transgender people are able to transition socially without surgery, that's wonderful and we make whatever practical changes are needed.

If they need to transition physically as well, then we provide love and support through the challenges of that. Diversity is celebrated everywhere in God's creation. In the person of Jesus, God became a human being and demonstrated God's welcome for the whole variety of global humanity and all forms of global life. That meant allowing himself to be brutally murdered and starting a whole new creation through his death and resurrection, and that love is our model.

(xiii) A conclusion

It's not enough for our churches just to accept LGBTQ people and show what would appear as tolerance. Without faith in and commitment to Christ as the only basis for church membership resulting in whole-hearted welcome, unity, and equality of love and respect for all who love and follow Jesus, we will continue to cause damage to the unity of the body of Christ and its witness to the world. We desperately need our LGBTQ brothers and sisters in our work of building God's new creation, and there is a whole global community to whom we need to reach out with love and share the good news of the gospel.

A number of things come together to show the need to love and welcome people from the LGBTQ community. There are, for example:

- Jesus's teaching and example on the supreme importance of love and inclusion;
- a modern, scientific understanding of natural orientation;
- awareness of the culture of exploitative and coercive social practices in biblical times;
- God's provision of supportive relationships as a human right;
- the need to see that social and cultural contexts can change the way we understand what was written in a very different context.
- we've a long way to go in celebrating God's passion for diversity that we see everywhere in our universe.

Further Discussion

1. Do the same sexual ethical principles apply equally to all, regardless of their identity?

2. The Anglican Church in Wales had a service in May 2024 to apologize for the ways Christians have hurt the LGBTQ community. Should we do the same?

3. Do you think it's fair to say that Paul, given his historical context, was probably condemning exploitation, coercion, and abuse, when he wrote negatively about sexual same-sex practices?

4. Should we welcome or disapprove of same-sex marriage?

5. Can we do more to support those questioning their gender identity?

2. Do the teaching and example of Jesus mean we should be pacifists?

In an increasingly dangerous world with so many violent conflicts, the idea that Christians should be pacifists is something that many of us seldom consider. The word "pacifism" was first used at an International Peace Conference in 1902, and it comes from the Latin words, *pax* meaning peace, and *faciens* meaning making. Even if pacifism is a relatively new word, the ideas behind it go back centuries and were adopted by movements such as the Anabaptist Mennonites and Amish, and perhaps most famously, by the Quakers.

Sydney Bailey, former Head of the Quaker United Nations Office and prolific writer on pacifism, is a good example of the Quaker approach to war. During World War Two, he was a conscientious objector, and worked with the Friends' Ambulance Unit, a volunteer ambulance unit set up by the Quakers. Jim Gee, spokesperson for the Quaker Peace Testimony, in his article, "Why I am still a pacifist," summed up Bailey's view of pacifism as threefold: refuse to kill, work to relieve suffering, and focus on peace-making.[24] "Work to relieve suffering" is a key aspect of pacifism, though imprisonment has prevented many from doing that during wartime.

An excellent entry on "Pacifism" by Andrew Faile in the Stanford Encyclopedia of Philosophy gives a good explanation of a wide range of types

24. Gee, "Why I am still a pacifist"

of pacifism. These are spread between two poles: absolute or contingent views about pacifism and maximal or minimal views of what should be called violence.

Absolute pacifists refuse the use of violence and war in all circumstances, including defence of your family or country, as well as self-defence. Their view of war is that in the long term, the negative effects of a war always outweigh anything war may achieve in the short term.

Contingent pacifists see the need for violence or war dependent on circumstances, as a last resort. Bertrand Russell found himself in this situation with the outbreak of World War Two. He was president of the Campaign for Nuclear Disarmament (CND) at the time, but he called himself a relative pacifist, because for Hitler to conquer Europe would be a far worse evil than waging war against him.

Maximal pacifists have a very extensive definition of the violence that they reject, and things like meat-eating and abortion may well be included. Minimal pacifists are willing to accept only certain types and uses of violence and war when absolutely needed. For instance, responding to a cruel tyrant with violence may justify some use of weaponry. CND, Greenpeace and the Greenham Common Women's Peace Camp (1981–2000) are good examples of non-violent fighting against specific types of violence.

Books like John Howard Yoder's *The Politics of Jesus*, and Jim Wallis's *The Soul of Politics*, focus on the social and therefore political implications of what we find in the life and example, the teaching, and the death and resurrection of Jesus. In Luke's gospel, Mary's song in response to the announcement that she is to give birth to Jesus sets out with great clarity her confidence that God's politics, and therefore Jesus's too, will always be to challenge the powerful and lift up the poor and the oppressed.[25] Zechariah, just informed that he would be the father of John who would prepare the way for the coming of God's Messiah, announces that as the last of the Old Testament prophets, John's job would be to "guide our feet into the path of peace."[26]

Jesus, before he began his ministry, spent forty days in the wilderness where he faced temptations about the work of building God's kingdom. In a future facing opposition from the defenders of the status quo, the power of Rome and of the Temple hierarchy, he rejected force as a way of achieving his kingship. Instead, his task was to preach good news to the poor,

25. Luke 1: 46–55
26. Luke 1:79

freedom for the prisoners, sight for the blind, release for the oppressed, and the Jubilee year of God's blessing.[27] These are the politics of Jesus that become the politics of all who follow him.

He died a revolutionary, and found his disciples whom he met on the road to Emmaus after his resurrection feeling devastated because they "had hoped he was the one who was going to redeem Israel."[28] The revolution of Jesus's politics involves asking forgiveness for his killers, but it is never passive acceptance of our human situation and its conflicts. It will always be the transformation of both personal and social life, for that is the only way to bring about long-term change.

There have been wonderful examples of peace-making in recent times. The Peace People Movement in Northern Ireland during the violence of the Troubles was led by courageous and determined peace-making women from both republican and unionist areas. They started grassroot marches for peace across Northern Ireland in response to some of the terrible suffering and killings of the 1970s, and two of them, Mairead Maguire and Betty Williams, received the Nobel Peace Prize in 1976.

There is also the wonderful example of the Christian and Moslem women in Maluku in Halmahera, Indonesia who risked their lives by meeting together and, in a situation of violence dominated by men, started a women's movement across the barricades that ultimately brought to an end the fierce ethnic and religious sectarian conflict and appalling atrocities of 1999–2002.

Our modern world desperately needs peacemakers. Jim Gee, in his article mentioned earlier, sees the invasion of Ukraine and the attempt to take over the country, as with so many similar situations in history, as a huge challenge for absolute pacifists, but he also points to the lack of creative peace-making efforts by the rest of the world to foresee and work to prevent what was going to happen. Skills of foresight, courage, determination, creativity, conflict resolution techniques, and negotiation techniques are not just for professionals, but important in settling disputes of all kinds.

Good examples of peace-making are described in *Liberating the Politics of Jesus: Renewing Peace Theology through the Wisdom of Women*, edited by Elizabeth Albrecht and Darryl Stephens, which aims to provide a "revisioning" of peace theology through the stories and the eyes of women doing peace-making in challenging parts of the world.

27. Luke 4: 18–19
28. Luke 24: 21

Linda Peachey, one of the contributors to the book, writes about involvement in "creative resistance to the powers of evil."[29] If the word "passive" gets associated with "pacifism," that's a major mistake because the two words, pacifism and passive have completely opposite meanings. To be passive means you're not active because some outer force is acting on you and preventing you from acting.

In the work of "disrupting cycles of violence," Elizabeth Albrecht, in her work with groups of women, calls for opportunities of truth telling and breaking the silence for victims, and for the cross of Jesus not to be seen as an example of silent acceptance of suffering, but as a constant reminder of transition to a new resurrected life.[30] Karen Guth calls for "revolutionary acts" of hospitality and sharing across all kinds of barriers, whether racial, social, or economic, because the key word in the Christian gospel is reconciliation, which becomes the key task of all who work for peace.[31]

When we look at the example and teaching of Jesus, we can have the highest regard for pacifist groups like the Quakers, the Amish and the Mennonites, and the millions of women and men who have struggled and suffered for the cause of peace rather than war. We could name some well-known pacifists like abolitionist and founder of the Society for the Promotion of Permanent and Universal Peace, Thomas Clarkson, Leo Tolstoy, Albert Schweitzer, Mahatma Gandhi, Martin Luther King, and Bertha van Sutter, the first woman to win the Nobel Peace Prize in 1889, with her novel *Lay Down Your Arms*. At the top of the list of those who laid down their lives for peace and reconciliation is, of course, Jesus, and through him has come the greatest gift of all, the resurrection to God's new creation, because Jesus died "to reconcile to himself all things, everything on earth and everything in heaven, making peace through his death on the cross." (Colossians 1:19–20).

Further Discussion

1. Is there a reason for followers of Christ to be pacifists?

2. Can you think of good examples of peace-making that you know about?

---

29. Albrecht & Stephens *Liberating the Politics*, ch.7
30. Albrecht & Stephens *Liberating the Politics*, ch.6
31. Albrecht & Stephens, *Liberating the Politics*, ch.4

3. What should our attitude be to other religions?

In St Peter's first letter, we are urged always to be ready to make our defence to anyone who demands an account of our hope, and to do it with gentleness and reverence. The words "gentleness and reverence" point us to a variety of moral, philosophical, theological, and practical reasons for taking care about how we consider and interact with other religions or belief systems. We are called to explain and defend the radical uniqueness of Jesus Christ and the good news of the gospel with a gentleness and reverence that ought to characterize all our relationships with those who differ from us. Gentleness (or meekness) is one of the fruits of the Spirit in Galatians 5, and it's a simple issue of politeness and civility to show humility and respect in dealing with other people's beliefs.

A second reason for acting with reverence in relation to other religions is expressed by Bruce Nicholls in his book, *Is Jesus the Only Way to God?* when he writes about the glimpses of grace that are found in other religions. A similar point was made by Oxford University friends and colleagues, J. R. R. Tolkien and C. S. Lewis. Tolkien found in the traditional human myths and stories that he knew so intimately, "a splintered fragment of the true light, the eternal truth that is with God."[32]

Lewis added the image of echoes as well as glimpses when he wrote that we shouldn't be surprised that the imaginations of pagan storytellers provide a glimpse into the "whole cosmic story - the theme of incarnation, death and rebirth."[33] Lewis's emphasis on desire or longing in *Surprised by Joy* develops his view of glimpses or echoes provided by God as signposts to what is ultimately true and revealed through Christ and his incarnation. Christianity is the fulfilment of what is hinted at in all the religions at their best, and it all comes into focus in the person of Jesus.[34]

A third reason for approaching other people's beliefs with meekness as well as respect is that the distinctive difference between Christianity and other religions is grace. The death of Jesus to redeem us is God's gift of love and grace, but grace is also God's providential love and benevolence to all people everywhere, whatever their religion or lack of religion.

A fourth reason for approaching other religions with respect or reverence is that we still have much to learn from them. Gerald McDermott

32. Carpenter, *J R R Tolkien*, 151

33. Lewis, *Screwtape Proposes*, 50

34. Lewis, *God in the Dock*, 138

in his book, *Can Evangelicals Learn from World Religions?*[35] claims that God has not left himself without a witness among non-Christian traditions.[36] The journey to belief can often involve learning from other great religious thinkers and traditions. MacDermott mentions Augustine and Neo-Platonism, Aquinas and Aristotle, Calvin and Renaissance humanism, as examples of thinkers and traditions that helped them more clearly understand God's revelation in Christ.

There remains a practical reason for developing our knowledge of other religions. If we are to explain and defend the gospel, it is important to do so with an understanding of other people's assumptions, approaches and beliefs. Introducing others to the good news of the gospel usually involves forming genuine and loving relationships with them. According to a recent religious knowledge survey in the USA, atheists, agnostics, Jews and Mormons outperformed Christians on questions about the core teachings, history and leading figures of major world religions.[37]

If this is true in a wider context, it is no wonder that many of us have few opportunities to demonstrate the love of God to those who hold other religious convictions. Few people change their beliefs through confrontation and disagreement. Harmony is a starting point and love and understanding provide a basis for relationship. Discrediting what other people believe tends to be counter-productive, and only makes people more determined to hold on to their own convictions. We're called to encourage people to ask questions when they see the attractiveness of what we do and say.

As we have seen, an approach to other religions characterized by gentleness and respect is not only morally and practically the right approach, but is also philosophically and theologically crucial.

Further Discussion

1. What should characterize our relationship with other religions?

2. What sort of things can we learn from other religions?

35. McDermott, *Can Evangelicals Learn*
36. Acts 14:17
37. Pew Research Center, "What Americans Know"

4. Could AI mean the end of humanity as we know it?

We know that our lives already have artificial intelligence embedded in them, and it's common to hear warnings that it's vital for humanity to develop a global agreement about its future directions and uses. Algorithms are already deciding what we hear or see on our social media and on our phones and laptops. We might say that power is moving from humans to algorithms, but that's not yet true. It's still small groups of humans who create and use the algorithms.

To adapt what C. S. Lewis wrote about the use of power when he was writing in 1943, power over AI still turns out to be power exercised by some people over other people with AI as its instrument. Lewis's argument was a defence of democracy, and opposition to all forms of tyranny with power in the hands of a few. Worst of all, he wrote, would be a theocracy, with an "inquisitor" who thinks his cruelty is a divinely ordained calling.[38]

It's not hard to see both the benefits and dangers of AI in the future. The benefits of being able to analyse unlimited amounts of data in milliseconds are obvious for business, for health and medicine and for research of all kinds. The dangers for human jobs, for warfare, for surveillance, for crime, for misinformation, for deep fakes, and for power in the hands of dictators are clear too. We can't stop the onrush of progress, but as with so many discoveries in the past, the sooner we achieve a global agreement on human and ethical values and principles about the uses of AI, the better. That won't stop dictators and villains doing whatever is possible for themselves, but at least it will make them open to condemnation.

The big threat about the future is what Stephen Hawking has warned in his book, *Brief Answers to Big Questions*.[39] What happens when "AI develops a will of its own . . . in conflict with ours?" Hawking was making a specific comment in the context of warfare and weapons. The question of AI developing consciousness like ours is a separate issue.

In relation to the danger of losing control over autonomous machines, as long ago as 2016, Bonnie Docherty, at Harvard Law School, was lead writer of a Human Rights Watch report called *Killer Robots and the Concept of Meaningful Human Control*. The report's concern, and Hawking's too, was robots making autonomous decisions about when and how to use "lethal, autonomous weapons systems" on land, on sea, and in the

38. Lewis, *Of This and Other Worlds*, 104–109
39. Hawking, *Brief Answers*, ch.9

air. Selecting targets and deciding to kill would no longer have any human agency and could be outside any human legal responsibility. It was urgent, said the report, for nations to come together and outlaw the use of such weapons.

Events since 2016 have shown how right the report was, but maybe also, how quickly events outstrip human good intentions to retain control. Global consensus has never been more essential if we are to survive with elements of our common humanity intact. *The Conversation* online has Docherty's impassioned summary of the report's main conclusions.[40]

In relation to AI developing a level of self-awareness that could be called consciousness, one answer is that consciousness remains the great mystery in neuroscience. We don't yet know how our awareness and experience of ourselves and the world we live in, our thoughts, our feelings and our sensory processes, have emerged from mindless matter, so it seems very unlikely for consciousness to create itself. For humans, the same cause can produce a vast number of conscious responses in different people, because human variables interact in unique ways. Rosalind Picard's book on affective computing was a launching pad for the ongoing development of AI systems that can recognize, interpret, process, and simulate human feelings and emotions, but the key word remains "simulate."[41]

Picard saw the benefits of enabling machines to recognize ways of understanding human emotions and use data input to respond to those emotions. However, the challenge is that in real life situations, we're hugely skilled at disguising our emotions through language, voice and facial expression. Another challenge is finding adequate algorithms to reduce or eliminate the inevitable biases in human data. Providing equality for each gender, each race and colour, and each age group in a job interview or application somehow has to depend on humans working out in advance what equality means in that context.

There remains a vast difference between human intelligence and artificial intelligence, between the human brain and the AI brain. Our own awareness of ourselves and the world around us changes from moment to moment in response to our thoughts, memories, emotional reactions and physical changes in our bodies. The idea that machines might acquire consciousness remotely similar to ours is still a realm of science fiction. Our individual consciousness is still so wonderful, so complex, so unique, that it

---

40. Docherty, "Losing Control"

41. Picard, *Affective Computing*

remains what distinguishes us as living beings. As I suggested in chapter 3, "Modern Science and Christian Faith," it's the greatest pointer to our being in the image of a personal creator God who wants to communicate and live in relationship with us.

Further Discussion

1. What makes you hopeful about the future with AI?

2. What makes you fearful about the future with AI?

3. Do you think there will ever be shared global regulations about the development and uses of AI?

5. What should characterize a Christian approach to immigration?

Let me respond by looking briefly at five aspects: some Christian principles about immigration, immigration as a gift as well as a challenge, the economic impact of immigration, Umberto Eco's warnings from his Italian experience of fascism, and some suggestions for improving an immigration policy.

Some principles

If you ever hear anyone claiming a connection between Christianity and complaints about immigration, there's one clear, consistent message throughout the whole Bible, and that's welcome and care for the stranger and the foreigner. That's especially true if they're migrants because of special need, whether it's because of war, persecution, poverty, or trafficking. Welcome, care, and love for migrants is the teaching and commandment of Jesus, the essence of the Christian gospel, demonstrated again and again in examples in the Bible, and is the law of God in the Old Testament Torah.

Christians follow Jesus Christ who:

- as a baby, was taken as a refugee to Egypt, because his life was in danger. He returned later to his homeland, but remained displaced and couldn't go back to his Judea home, because Herod's son was in charge there, and the family settled in Nazareth in Galilee.

- identified himself with all strangers and foreigners: "When did we see you a stranger and invite you in, or needing clothes and clothe you? The King will reply, 'Truly I tell you, whatever you did for one of the least of these brothers and sisters of mine, you did for me.'"[42]

- had an ancestor called Ruth who was from Moab, a hated enemy of Israel, but when she arrived in Israel accompanying her mother-in-law, Naomi, she found acceptance, was cared and provided for, and eventually became a blood-ancestor not just of King David, but also of Jesus, the Messiah.

- came to live among us by his incarnation as the son of God, allowing us to find God's blessing on our lives by welcoming, receiving, and loving him.

- gave us his great twofold commandment: "Love the Lord your God with all your heart, and with all your soul, and with all your mind, and with all your strength. The second is this: 'Love your neighbor as yourself. There is no commandment greater than these."[43]

Christians believe in a God who:

- calls for love to be put into action and "loves the foreigners residing among you, giving them food and clothing. And you are to love those who are foreigners, for you yourselves were foreigners in Egypt."[44]

- "watches over the foreigner, and sustains the fatherless and the widow."[45]

- sets clear instructions: "When a foreigner resides among you in your land, do not mistreat them. The foreigner residing among you must be treated as your native-born. Love them as yourself, for you were foreigners in Egypt. I am the Lord your God."[46]

42. Matt 25: 38–40
43. Mark 12: 30–31
44. Deut 10: 18–19
45. Ps 146: 6 & 9
46. Lev 19: 33–34

- gives blessing on those who put his love into action: "Bring all the tithes of that year's produce and store it in your towns, so that . . . the foreigners . . . who live in your towns may come and eat and be satisfied, and so that the Lord your God may bless you in all the work of your hands."[47]

- will one day call all of us to account for how we put his love into action.

- will one day unite all of us as one family in his new earth.

Christians believe in God's Holy Spirit who:

- inspired the apostle Paul to understand the universal inclusiveness of the gospel and of the love of God: "There is neither Jew nor Gentile, neither slave nor free, nor is there male and female, for you are all one in Christ Jesus."[48]

- brings the good news of God's love, grace, and forgiveness to all people throughout the world.

- travels with us in all our journeys through life.

- calls on us to love and care, following the example and command of our saviour, Jesus.

A challenge and a gift

We've had decades of talk about the problem of immigration in the UK. The focus has almost always been on the problems and challenges for those who receive migrants. There is pressure on social and physical infrastructure, on natural resources, and on providing housing, schooling, and working opportunities without disadvantaging those in the receiving community who struggle to meet their own needs. Integration will always be hard work on both sides. Love always recognizes a cost. We shouldn't fall into what economist J. K. Galbraith called "one of man's oldest exercises in moral philosophy; the search for a superior moral justification for selfishness."[49]

---

47. Deut 14: 28–29
48. Gal 3: 28
49. Galbraith, "Wealth and Poverty"

Migrants have lived with huge problems. Many have had to face leaving the only home they have known, with few or no possessions, and making an agonizing journey that they might or might not survive, with no idea what lies ahead. They need to be enabled to struggle with their experiences in a context of care and compassion. Too often, after all they've been through, they experience rejection and hate.

As well as economic benefits discussed below, immigration can supply gaps in the labour market, bring new energy, fresh thinking, and encourage cultural diversity. It has always puzzled me that anyone who believes in God as creator of our universe doesn't look around, and see colour and diversity as the characteristics that most obviously delight the creator.

The foreword to the publication, *Love the Stranger*, from the Catholic Church's 2023 Bishops of England and Wales Conference, emphasizes the gifts that immigrants bring us. Our calling as Christians is to a love that is "unequivocal and indiscriminate." We have the opportunity for a huge learning experience from encounter with them and their stories, developing our global understanding. We have opportunities to demonstrate our oneness with Christ in service and in prayer, and where possible celebrate, develop, and share our faith. *Love the Stranger* goes on to set out twenty-four key principles in our response to immigrants.[50]

Economic aspects

There are things we can say with some confidence about the economic effect of immigration in general, given that immigration includes all migrants who were born in a different country, whether they are highly-skilled or low-skilled, whether they are asylum-seekers or students, whether they are temporary or permanent.

Two conclusions about immigration in general seem clear. A recent study by the Institute for Fiscal Studies in the UK confirmed that, in the long term, "immigrants are large net fiscal contributors."[51] A University of Notre Dame study on the impact of immigration in the USA found the same conclusion. Most refugees ultimately become net fiscal contributors. "By twenty years after arrival, the average refugee adult has contributed approximately $21,000 more in taxes at all levels than the combined cost

50. Catholic Bishops, "The Gift of Migration"
51. Dustmann, *Inequality*, p.35

of governmental expenditures on their behalf, including the cost of initial resettlement."[52]

Second, governments constantly emphasize economic growth as the key to prosperity. In their 2023 study of *The Macroeconomic Effects of Large Immigration Waves*, the International Monetary Fund found "no evidence of negative effects on aggregate employment of the native-born population." It's important to provide access for the immigrant community to the labor market. Otherwise, we "substantially reduce their possibilities to contribute to their host economy." Overall, "we find positive and sizable effects of large waves of immigration on total-factor productivity."[53] The conclusion for the USA is clear: "the immigrant community bolsters our economies at federal, state, and local levels."[54]

That leaves open whether we should take pride in the immigration of highly-skilled people who are a loss to the countries they leave behind. Many people seem to have no problem with that moral question, but, on the contrary, they have a problem with our taking people purely for humanitarian reasons. These are people who come as asylum-seekers to escape war, persecution, or extreme poverty and danger. Of course there's a cost to that, but that's the meaning of being humanitarian, and seeing our responsibility to be involved in making the world a better place for our whole human family to live in. But when we consider the cost, it's easy to forget that, in the longer term, these people also contribute to our lives economically, as well as in so many other ways, as we saw when speaking of them as a gift to us.

One of the few studies I can find online that wrestles with the issue of the long-term economic contribution of those in great need of help and support, but with limited skills to offer, is the recent World Bank report, "Threat or Help? The Effects of Unskilled Immigrant Workers on National Productivity Growth." The report argues that "while unskilled immigrant workers have relatively low formal human capital, theory suggests that they can still contribute to productivity improvements."[55]

Many research studies have shown a small initial cost to native-born low-wage workers facing competition from low-skilled immigrants,

---

52. Evans, "Economic Benefits"

53. Engler, "Macroeconomic Effects" p.15. Total-factor productivity measures growth by relating total productivity output to the total inputs used.

54. Engler, *Macroeconomic Effects* p.2

55. Devadas, "Threat or Help?" p.1

although medium and high-paid native workers are likely to gain. However, if you read that World Bank article, you'll find that it suggests at least a dozen indirect contributions with which unskilled immigrants can not only enhance productivity, but also provide indirect contributions to the native work force.[56]

Perhaps the most telling point about immigration and the economy is in the UK Institute for Fiscal Studies report mentioned earlier. As well as finding that "the effects of immigration on inequality in the UK were very small,"[57] their research came to a significant conclusion that perceptions about the impact of immigration on economic factors can be "mostly attributed to racial and cultural concerns, rather than perceived economic competition."[58]

Umberto Eco and warnings about fascism.

Umberto Eco, the great Italian writer and novelist, was born in 1932 and grew up under Mussolini and Italian Fascism. One of the lessons he learnt and has passed on to every generation was that fascism reappears in many forms and we will always need to keep alert to ensure our democracies aren't taken over by totalitarianism. Eco listed fourteen generic features of Fascism.[59] I've summarized seven of them below. If they don't scare us, then maybe we haven't been paying attention. Eco died in 2016, and saw the beginnings of social media, but the ways in which social media are being used to achieve the features below today wouldn't have surprised him.

- "Fascism is racist by definition." Power demands the unity of a variety of social classes to meet what they see as the threat of foreigners who weren't born in our country and bring a culture that is different.

- "Fascism speaks Newspeak," (the language of the rulers in Orwell's *1984.*) The aim is to limit opportunities for complex and critical reasoning and discussion. Just do what you're told. Vocabulary and syntax are simple and clear as well as violent.

56. Devadas, "Threat or Help?" pp.2–4
57. Dustmann, *Inequality*, p.35
58. Dustmann, *Inequality*, p.2
59. Eco, *Ur-Fascism.*

- A cult of action for action's sake. Mobilize for action and the use of force. Action needs no previous reflection, because intellectualism is an enemy that gets in the way of action.

- "Contempt for the weak." We belong to the best people of the world, and our leaders are the best among the citizens.

- "We are the Voice of the People." The emotional response of a select small group of citizens is presented and insisted on as the Voice of the People.

- "Obsession with a plot." The followers must feel besieged. The easiest way to deal with the plot is xenophobia, machismo, and violence.

- "Social frustration." Our enemies are out to humiliate us but they will never succeed, and we want all social classes to work together.

Eco ended his essay by adapting Franklin Roosevelt's 1938 radio address: "I venture the challenging statement that if American democracy ceases to move forward as a living force, seeking day and night by peaceful means to better the lot of our citizens, Fascism . . . will grow in strength in our land."[60]

Some suggestions to improve an immigration policy.

- Serious involvement towards helping address the causes of migration: foreseeing and working to avoid conflict and war; control of the arms trade; mobilizing aid and trade to address poverty, working hard to address climate change, and working to support global human rights.

- A change of language in talking about immigration. Emphasis on the contributions and gifts that all immigrants can bring, and the positive aspects as well as the challenges.

- We need secure borders for protective reasons, but common sense tells us the importance of safe routes so that people in need can come legally, and speedy processing of all who arrive. Reuniting split families is in everyone's interest

- A proper integration programme, so that immigrants quickly become active participants in all areas of social life and work, and their contributions welcomed.

60. Roosevelt, "Radio Address."

- Recognition that we need to address speedily our national failures in providing adequate housing, educational, and health resources.

- Our churches and all community groups mobilized to support newcomers. Churches might be interested in "The Immigrants' Creed" from the 2018 edition of the *Book of Common Worship*, compiled by the Office of Theology and Worship for the Presbyterian Church (U.S.A.), and available online.[61]

Further Discussion:

1. Which of the biblical examples given here do you see as particularly meaningful to you as you reflect on welcoming the stranger?

2. What would you suggest as ways to support and include immigrant people or groups in the community that you belong to?

3. Are there examples of racist attitudes and behaviour that you have noticed or experienced in your community or work place?

4. How can we make social media safer and more positive places?

61. Office of Theology, *Book of Common Worship*

Bibliography

Albrecht, Elizabeth, and Darryl Stephens, eds. *Liberating the Politics of Jesus: Renewing Peace Theology through the Wisdom of Women*. London: T. & T. Clark, 2020.

Anderson, Norman. *Christianity: The Witness of History*. Carol Stream, IL: Tyndale, 1969.

Arnold, Brian. "Born into the Greco-Roman World." https://ps.edu>born-into-the-greco-roman-world

Asprou, Helena. "Music is a universal language, new Harvard University study proves."https://www.classicfm.com/music-news/study-proves-music-is-universal-language/

Atkinson, David. "Why we in the churches need to treat climate change more urgently." http://operationnoah.org/wp-content/uploads/2015/02/Climate-and-Gospel-David-Atkinson-30-01-2015.pdf

Bacon, Francis. *The Advancement of Learning*. London: Cassell & Company, 1893.

Barth, Karl. *Church Dogmatics, II. 1* "The Doctrine of God," ed. Thomas F. Torrance and Geoffrey W. Bromiley. Translated by T. H. L. Parker and W. B. Johnston, et al. Edinburgh: T&T Clark, 1957.

———. *Come Holy Spirit: Sermons*. Translated by George W. Richards, Elmer G. Homrighausen, & Karl J, Ernst. New York, Round Table, 1933.

———. *Dogmatics in Outline*. Translated by G. T. Thomson. New York: Philosophical Library, 1949.

Bartholomew, Craig, and Michael Goheen. *The Drama of Scripture: Finding Our Place in the Biblical Story*. Grand Rapids, MI: Baker Academic, 2014.

Baulkham, Richard. *Bible and Mission: Christian Witness in a Postmodern World*. Milton Keynes: Paternoster, 2003.

Bell, Rob. *Love Wins*. Glasgow: Harper Collins, 2012.

Berenbaum, Michael. "Elie Wiesel, the Moral Force Who Made Sure We Will Never Forget Evil of Holocaust." https://forward.com/news/344179/elie-wiesel-the-moral-force-who-made-sure-we-will-never-forget-evil-of-holo/

Berry, R. J. *Christians and Evolution: Christian Scholars Change Their Minds*. London: Monarch, 2014.

———. "Creation and Evolution, Not Creation or Evolution." Faraday Paper 12, https://www.faraday.cam.ac.uk/wp content/uploads/resources/Faraday%20Papers

———. *Creation, Evolution and the Bible*. Vancouver: Regent College Publishing, 2004.

———. "The Cursed Earth: Is the Fall Credible?" Christians in Science, https://www.cis.org.uk/serve.php?filename=scb-11-1-berry.pdf

Bibliography

BioLogos. "Asking Questions of Our Faith." https://biologos.org/articles/rachel-held-evans-1981–2019-asking-questions-of-our-faith
———. "God's Word, God's World," https://biologos.org/
———. "How could humans have evolved and still be in the image of God?" https://biologos.org/
———. "Is Animal Suffering Part of God's Good Creation?" https://biologos.org/
Bishop of Truro. *Independent Review for the Foreign Secretary of FCO Support for Persecuted Christians.* https://christianpersecutionreview.org.uk/interim-report/ 2019.
Blake, William. *The Poetical Works of William Blake.* ed. John Sampson. London: Oxford University Press, 1914
———. *William Blake Poems & Prophecies.* ed. MaxPlowman, Max. London: Dent, 1927.
Blocher, Henri. *Evil and the Cross: An Analytical Look at the Problem of Pain.* Translated by David G. Preston. Grand Rapids, MI: Kregel, 2004.
Boda, Mark. *The NIV Application Commentary: Haggai & Zechariah.* Grand Rapids, MI: Zondervan, 2004.
Boyd, Gregory. *God of the Possible: A Biblical Introduction to the Open View of God.* Ada, MI: Baker, 2000.
Bruce, F. F. *The New Testament Documents: Are They Reliable?* London: IVP, 2000.
Brueggemann, Walter. "The Book of Amos shows how God's emancipatory embrace includes LGBTQ people." https://outreach.faith/2023/04/walter-brueggemann-the-book-of-amos-shows-how-gods-emancipatory-embrace-includes-lgbtq-people/
Buechner, Frederick. *Wishful Thinking: A Theological ABC.* New York: Harper & Row, 1973.
Burnett, Gary. *Paul Distilled.* Eugene, OR: Wipf & Stock, 2021.
Burroughs, Dillon, "The Resurrection Accurately Recorded and Reported." https://jashow.org/articles/the-resurrection-accurately-recorded-and-reported/
Carpenter, Humphrey. *J. R. R. Tolkien: A Biography.* London: George Allen & Unwin, 1977.
Carter, R. *Language and Creativity: The Art of Common Talk.* Abingdon-on-Thames: Routledge, 2004.
Casal, Jose Luis. "The Immigrants' Creed." https://www.discipleshomemissions.org/wp-content/uploads/2017/05/Immigrants-Creed-Jose-Luis-Casal.pdf
Catholic Bishops' Conference of England and Wales. "The gift of migration." https://www.cbcew.org.uk/love-the-stranger-gift-of-migration/
Church of Ireland General Synod. *Standing Committee Sub–Committee on Sectarianism Report.* https://www.ireland.anglican.org/resources/46/church-of-ireland-general-synod 1999.
Ciardi, John. *Manner of Speaking.* Rutgers Univ. Press, New Brunswick, N.J., 1972.
Clarkson, Joel. "Three Ways Creativity Connects Us with the Creator." https://relevantmagazine.com/faith/three-ways-creativity-connects-the-created-with-the-creator/
Collier, Winn. *A Burning in My Bones: The Authorised Biography of Eugene H. Peterson.* Colorado Springs: Waterbrook, 2021.
Collins, Francis. *The Language of God.* London: Simon & Schuster, 2007.
Community of the Resurrection. *Mirfield Mission Hymn Book.* Mirfield, CR, 1922
Conradie, E. *Resurrection, Finitude and Ecology.* In T. Peters, T. R. J. Russell & M. Welker, *Resurrection: Theological and Scientific Assessments,* Grand Rapids, MI: Eerdmans, 2002, 277–296.

Bibliography

Corey, S. M. "Science, Philosophy and Religion: A Symposium." *Journal of Educational Psychology*. 32:3 (1941) 228–29.

Cottrell-Boyce, F. *God on Trial*. London: Hat Trick Productions, 2008.

———. "Losing My Religion." *The Guardian*, 19 August 2008.

Craig, William Lane. "Primacy of the New Testament Documents." https://www.cbn.com/special/apologetics/articles/primacy-of-new-testament.aspx

———. *Time and Eternity: Exploring God's Relationship to Time*. Wheaton, IL: Crossway, 2001.

Critchlow, Stephen. *Mindful of the Light: Practical Help and Spiritual Hope for Mental Health*. Instant Apostle, Watford, 2016.

Crump, David. *Knocking on Heaven's Door: A New Testament Theology of Petitionary Prayer*. Grand Rapids, MI: Baker Academic, 2006.

Davies, Paul. *Superforce*. London: Simon & Schuster, 1984.

Davis, Hunter. "A Biblical Perspective on Immigration." https://worldrelief.org/dublog-a-biblical-perspective-on-immigration

Devadas, Sharmila. "Threat or Help? The Effects of Unskilled Immigrant Workers on National Productivity Growth." Research & Policy Brief from the World Bank Malaysia Hub, https://documents1.worldbank.org/curated/en/693241488820573902/pdf/Threat-or-help-the-effects-of-unskilled-immigrant-workers-on-national-productivity-growth.pdf

Dennett, Daniel. *Darwin's Dangerous Idea: Evolution and the Meanings of Life*. London: Simon & Schuster, 1995.

Dickinson, Emily. *Poems, Third Series, XLIII*. ed. M. L. Todd, Amherst: 1896. https://www.gutenberg.org/files/12242/12242-h/12242-h.htm

Docherty, Bonnie. "Losing control: The dangers of killer robots." https://theconversation.com/losing-control-the-dangers-of-killer-robots-58262

Dostoevsky, Fyodor. *The Brothers Karamazov*. London: Penguin Classics, 1958.

Dustmann, C., Kastis, Y. and Preston, I. *Inequality and Immigration*, Institute for Fiscal Studies Deaton Review of Inequalities, 2022.

Eco, Umberto. "Ur-Fascism. Freedom and liberation are an unending task." *New York Review of Books*, June 22, 1995, https://www.nybooks.com/articles/1995/06/22/ur-fascism/

The Ecumenical Review. "God's Gift and Call to Unity—and Our Commitment." https://onlinelibrary.wiley.com/doi/abs/10.1111/erev.12064

Edwards, Jonathan. *Basic Writings*, ed. Ola Elizabeth Winslow. New York: The New American Library, 1978.

Einstein, Albert. "Science and Religion," In *Ideas and Opinions*. New York: Citadel Press, 1956.

Engler, Philipp, Margaux MacDonald, Roberto Piazza, Galen Sher. "The Macroeconomic Effects of Large Immigration Waves." *International Monetary Fund Working Paper*, WP/23/259, 2023, https://www.imf.org/en/Publications/WP/Issues/2023/12/14/The-Macroeconomic-Effects-of-Large-Immigration-Waves-542526

European Space Agency. https://www.esa.int/Science/Space/Planct/

Evans, Rachel Held. "15 reasons I left church" and "15 reasons I stayed with the church." https://rachelheldevans.com/blog/15-reasons-i-left-church#google_vignette

———. *Faith Unraveled: How a Girl Who Knew All the Answers Learned to Ask Questions*. Grand Rapids, MI: Zondervan, 2014.

Evans, Richard. *The Anatomy of Hell*. New York: Farrar, Straus and Giroux, 2015.

Bibliography

Evans, William. "Economic benefits of admitting refugees outweigh costs." *Notre Dame News*, https://news.nd.edu/news/economic-benefits-of-admitting-refugees-outweigh -costs/

Farrar, Austin. *Love Almighty and Ills Unlimited*. London: Collins, 1961.

Ferguson, James. "Open Secrets: The Gospel, Nature, and Poetry." In Pamela Ferguson, *Poetry of Nature and Grace*, Eugene, OR: Resource 68–78, 2023.

Ferguson, James et al. *Unlocking Creativity in Literacy. Report to the Northern Ireland Literacy Steering Group*. Belfast: Stranmillis University College, 2005.

Ferguson, Pamela. *From Shore to Shore: Life in God's Global Kingdom: Reflections in Poetry and Prose*. Eugene, OR: Resource, 2020.

Fiala, Andrew. "Pacifism." Stanford Encyclopedia of Philosophy, https://plato.stanford. edu/entries/pacifism/

Flew, Antony. *Has Science Discovered God?* DVD Set, 2004.

Foster, Richard. *Celebration of Discipline*. New York: Harper & Row, 1978.

Frackowiak, R et al. *Human Brain Function*. Cambridge, MA: Academic Press, 2004.

Freiberger, Marianne. "The multiverse: science or speculation?" https://plus.maths.org/ content/cosmology-science-or-speculation

Friends of the Earth. "Coronavirus: a green and fair recovery plan." https:// friendsoftheearth.uk/climate-change/how-uk-government-can-tackle-climate

Galbraith, J. K. "Wealth and Poverty." *Congressional Record*, Vol. 109, Senate, 18 Dec 1963.

Galileo Galilei. *The Assayer*. Translated by Stillman Drake. Philadelphia, University of Pennsylvania Press, 2016.

Gee, Jim. "Why I am still a pacifist." https://www.quaker.org.uk/blog/why-i-am-still-a-pacifist

Gleghorn, Michael. "Ancient Evidence for Jesus from Non-Christian Sources." https:// www.bethinking.org/jesus/ancient-evidence-for-jesus-from-non-christian-sources

Glendalough Hermitage Centre. "Spirituality." https://glendaloughhermitage.ie/

Guite, Malcolm. "After Prayer: Lent with George Herbert." https://malcolmguite. wordpress.com/2020/02/27/after-prayer-lent-with-george-herbert-day-1/

———. *Faith, Hope and Poetry: Theology and the Poetic Imagination*. London: Routledge, 2016.

Gunton, Colin. *Christ and Creation*. Milton Keynes: Paternoster, 1992.

Haensly & Reynolds. *Handbook of Creativity*. New York: Plenum, 1989.

Hawking, Stephen. *Brief Answers to the Big Questions*. London: John Murray, 2018.

Hawking, Stephen and Thomas Hertog. "Populating the Landscape: A Top-Down Approach." https://www.arxiv-vanity.com/papers/hep-th/0602091/

Heaney, Seamus. *Crediting Poetry: The Nobel Lecture*. Oldcastle, Meath, Gallery, 1995.

Herbert, George. *The Temple*. Cambridge, Thomas Buck, 1633.

Hick, John. *Evil and the God of Love*. New York: Harper & Row, 1978.

Hilborn, David, ed. *The Nature of Hell. A Report by the Evangelical Alliance Commission on Unity and Truth among Evangelicals*. Carlisle: Paternoster, 2000.

Human Rights Watch. *Killer Robots and the Concept of Meaningful Human Control*. https://www.hrw.org/news/2016/04/11/killer-robots-and-concept-meaningful-human control 2016.

Huntingdon's Chapels. *Select Collection of Hymns*. London: Hughes & Walsh, 1780

Industrial Workers of the World. *Little Red Songbook*. Spokane, Washington: 1911.

Isaac, Shirley. "God-Language and Gender: Some Trinitarian Reflections." https:// directionjournal.org/29/2/god-language-and-gender-some-trinitarian.html

Jackson, Robert. *Religious Education: An Interpretive Approach.* London: Hodder and Stoughton, 1997.

John, Yohan. "Why Science Will Probably Never Address the Problem of Consciousness." https://www.forbes.com/sites/quora/2016/09/16/why-science-will-probably-never-address-the-problem-of-consciousness/?sh=37d6991b654b

Johnson, Darrell. *Experiencing the Trinity.* Vancouver: Regent College Publishing, 2002.

Jones, T. P. *Creative Learning in Perspective.* University of London Press, 1972.

Josephus. "Account of Jesus." https://www.josephus.org/testimonium.htm

Julian of Norwich. *Revelations of Divine Love.* Translated by Barry Windeatt. Oxford University Press, 2015.

Kimel, Aidan. "The Universalist Hope in the Early Church." https://afkimel.wordpress.com/2014/05/21/the-universalist-hope-in-the-early-church/

Lefebvre, Michael. "I Am Who I Am. The Real Meaning of God's Name in Exodus." https://theaquilareport.com/i-am-who-i-am-the-real-meaning-of-gods-name-in-exodus/

Lennox, John. *Can Science Explain Everything?* London: The Good Book Company, 2019.

———. *God's Undertaker: Has Science Buried God?* Oxford: Lion, 2009.

Lewis, C. S. *The Abolition of Man.* Oxford University Press, 1943.

———. *Fern-seed and Elephants and Other Essays on Christianity,* ed. Walter Hooper. London: Fontana, 1975.

———. *God in the Dock: Essays on Theology and Ethics.* Ed. Walter Hooper. Grand Rapids, MI: Eerdmans, 1994.

———. *The Last Battle.* London, Collins, 1956.

———. *Mere Christianity.* London: Collins, 2012.

———. *Of This and Other Worlds: Essays and Stories,* ed. Walter Hooper. London: Collins, 1982.

———. *Reflections on the Psalms.* London: Collins, 1958.

———. *Screwtape Proposes a Toast and Other Pieces.* Oxford: Fount, 1974.

Licona, Michael. "What are the Primary Sources for Jesus' Resurrection?" https://hbu.edu/news-and-events/2016/06/03/primary-sources-jesuss-resurrection/

Livio, Mario. *Is God a Mathematician?* Ada, MI: Simon & Schuster, 2010.

Loader, William. "Same-sex relationships: A 1st-century perspective." https://researchportal.murdoch.edu.au/esploro/outputs/journalArticle/Same-sex-relationships-A-1st-century-perspective

Longfellow, Henry Wadsworth. *Outre-Mer: A Pilgrimage Beyond the Sea.* New York, Harper, 1835.

Lyotard, Jean-François. *The Postmodern Condition.* Manchester University Press, 1984.

McDermott, Gerald. *Can Evangelicals Learn from World Religions?* London: IVP, 2000.

MacDonald, Gregory. *The Evangelical Universalist.* London: SPCK, 2008.

McDowell. Josh. *The New Evidence that Demands a Verdict.* Edinburgh: Nelson, 1999.

McGrath, Alister. *Enriching Our Vision of Reality.* London: SPCK, 2016.

———. *The Open Secret: A New Vision for Natural Theology.* Oxford: Blackwell, 2008.

McLaren, Brian. *Do I Stay Christian? A Guide for the Doubters, the Disappointed, and the Disillusioned.* New York: St. Martin's Essentials, 2022.

———. *A Generous Orthodoxy.* Grand Rapids, MI: Zondervan, 2004.

Messer, Neil. "Evolution and Theodicy: How (not) to do science and theology." *Zygon: Journal of Religion and Science,* 53:3 (2018) 821–35.

Mill, J. S. *Nature, The Utility of Religion and Theism.* London: Rationalist Press, 1904.

Bibliography

Millar, Roy. *Come and See: An Invitation to Journey with Jesus and his Beloved Disciple John*. Revised Edition. Watford: Instant Apostle, 2020.

Moltmann, Jurgen. *The Coming of God: Christian Eschatology*. Translated Margaret Kohl. Minneapolis, MN, Fortress, 2004.

Morison. Frank. *Who Moved the Stone?* Notre Dame, IN: Christian Classics, 2017.

Mullins, Matthew. *Enjoying the Bible: Literary Approaches to Loving the Scriptures*. Grand Rapids MI, Baker Academic, 2019.

Music and Dancing. "The dance of love: Perichoresis." https://musicanddancing. wordpress.com

National Aeronautics and Space Administration. "ΛCDM Model of Cosmology." https:// lambda.gsfc.nasa.gov/education/graphic_history/univ_evol.html

Natural Resources Defense Council. "The Ecological Importance of Predators." https:// www.nrdc.org/sites/default/files/predatorimportance.pdf

National Health Service. "Gender dysphoria." https://www.nhs.uk/conditions/gender-dysphoria/

New Catholic Encyclopedia. "Aeon (in the Bible)." Encyclopedia.com. https://www. encyclopedia.com/religion/encyclopedias-almanacs-transcripts-and-maps/aeon-bible

Nicholls, Bruce. *Is Jesus the Only Way to God?* Auckland, NZ: Castle, 1967.

Nouwen, Henri. *Reaching Out: Three Movements of the Spiritual Life*. Cincinnati, OH: St. Anthony Messenger Press, 2006.

Office of Theology and Worship for the Presbyterian Church (U.S.A.). *Book of Common Worship*. Westminster John Knox Press 2018, https://worship.calvin.edu/resources/resource-library/the-immigrants-creed/

Oswalt, John. *The NIV Application Commentary: Isaiah*. Grand Rapids, MI: Zondervan 2003.

Parry, R. and C. Partridge, eds. *Universal Salvation? The Current Debate*. Milton Keynes: Paternoster, 2003.

Peacocke, Arthur. *Paths From Science Towards God*. Grantham: One World, 2001.

Pew Research Center. "What Americans Know About Religion." https://www.pewforum. org/2019/07/23/what-americans-know-about-religion/

Picard, Rosalind. *Affective Computing*. Cambridge: MIT Press, 2000.

Pinnock, Clark. *Flame of Love: A Theology of the Holy Spirit*. Illinois: IVP, 1996.

Pinnock, Clark et al, *The Openness of God: A Biblical Challenge to the Traditional Understanding of God*. London: IVP, 1994.

Piper, John. "God Filled Your Bible with Poems." https://www.desiringgod.org/articles/god-filled-your-bible-with-poems

Pliny the Younger. "Letters 10.96.1–7." https://biblicalscholarship.wordpress. com/2023/05/13/pliny-the-younger-letters-10-96-97/

Polkinghorne John and Nicholas Beale. *Questions of Truth*. Louisville: Westminster John Knox, 2009.

Polkinghorne, John. *Science and Providence: God's Interaction with the World*. London: SPCK, 2005.

―――. *Science and Religion in Quest of Truth*. London: SPCK, 2011.

Popper, Karl. "Natural Selection and the Emergence of Mind." Dialectica Vol.32, No.3/4 (1978) 339–55.

Rana, Fazale. "Animal Death Prevents Ecological Meltdown." https://reasons.org/explore/publications/connections/animal-death-prevents-ecological-meltdown

Bibliography

Reformed Church in America Commission on Worship. "The Theology and Place of Music in Worship." https://www.faithward.org/the-theology-and-place-of-music-in-worship/

Roa, Brittany Noelle. "Quantum Physics: The Bridge Between Science and Religion?" https://medium.com/the-ascent/quantum-physics-the-bridge-between-science-and-religion-2d4456c91763

Rockström, Johan. "Earth Day." *The Guardian*, 22 April, 2020.

Rohr, Richard. "The Early Eastern Church." Center for Action and Contemplation. https://cac.org/daily-meditations/early-eastern-church-2015-05-01/

———. "Universal Restoration." Center for Action and Contemplation. https://cac.org/daily-meditations/universal-restoration-2018-09-13/

———. *The Universal Christ*. London: SPCK, 2019.

Roosevelt. Franklin. "Radio Address on the Election of Liberals." 1938, https://www.presidency.ucsb.edu/documents/radio-address-the-election-liberals

Ross, Hugh. "The Creator and the Cosmos." https://www.leaderu.com/science/ross-justright.html

Sachs, Jonathan. "'The Chief Rabbi on Genesis." https://www.thejc.com/judaism/books/the-chief-rabbi-on-genesis

Schopenhauer, A. *On the Suffering of the World*. Translated by R. J. Hollingdale. London: Penguin Great Ideas, 2014.

Science Council. "Our definition of science." https://sciencecouncil.org/about-science/our-definition-of-science/#:~:text=Science%20is%20the%20pursuit%20and,Evidence

Scott & Sadie: "Eastern Christianity—Apokatastasis –The Restoration of All Things - Father Richard Rohr." https://scottandsadie.wordpress.com/2018/09/13/eastern-christianity-apokatastasis-the-restoration-of-all-things-father-richard-rohr/

Senz, Nicholas. "St. Luke got the greatest interview of all time." https://aleteia.org/2018/10/18/st-luke-got-the-greatest-interview-of-all-time/

Seth, Anil. *Being You: A New Science of Consciousness*. London: Faber, 2021.

Smith, Graeme. *Was the Tomb Empty?* London: Monarch, 2014.

Southgate, Christopher. *The Groaning of Creation: God, Evolution, and the Problem of Evil*. Louisville: Westminster John Knox, 2008.

St Basil the Great. "On Giving Thanks to the Creator." https://orthodoxchurchquotes.wordpress.com/category/sayings-from-saints-elders-and-fathers/st-basil-the-great/

St Francis of Assisi Parish. "Literary Styles in the Bible." https://stfrncis.org/bible-study/how-to-read-the-bible-2

Stott, John. *The Cross of Christ*. London: IVP, 2012.

Strobel, Lee. "Post." https://twitter.com/leestrobel/status/944981555587506176?lang=en

Suetonius. *Life of Nero*. https://penelope.uchicago.edu/Thayer/E/Roman/Texts/Suetonius/12Caesars/Nero*.html

Sutter, Bertha. *Lay Down Your Arms*. London: Longmans Green and Co., 1906.

Sutter, Paul. "What is quantum entanglement?" https://www.livescience.com/what-is-quantum-entanglement.html

Swain, Scott. "Is the Trinity in Genesis 1?" https://www.thegospelcoalition.org/article/trinity-genesis-1/

Talbott, Thomas. *The Inescapable Love of God*. Eugene, OR: Wipf & Stock, 2014.

Tegmark, Mark. *Our Mathematical Universe: My Quest for the Ultimate Nature of Reality*. London: Knopf Doubleday, 2014.

Bibliography

Tetlow, Joseph. "The Language of the Cross." https://www.ignatianspirituality.com/
ignatian-prayer/the-spiritual-exercises/the-language-of-the-cross/

Tozer, A.W. *The Attributes of God.* Volume 2, Chicago: Moody, 1997.

Twain, Mark. "The Pudd'nhead Maxims," in *Pudd'nhead Wilson's New Calendar.* New
York: Harper & Brothers, 1911.University College London. "Mammal diversity
exploded immediately after dinosaur Extinction." https://www.ucl.ac.uk/news/2015/
dec/mammal-diversity-exploded-immediately-after-dinosaur-extinction

Vanstone, W.H. *Love's Endeavour, Love's Expense.* London: Darton, Longman & Todd,
1977.

Wallace, Daniel. "A Brief Note on a Textual Problem in 2 Peter 3:10." https://bible.org/
article/brief-note-textual-problem-2-peter-3:10

Wallis, Jim. *The Soul of Politics: A Practical and Prophetic Vision for Change.* London:
Fount, 1994.

Ward, Keith. *The Big Questions in Science and Religion.* Conshohocken, PA: Templeton,
2008.

Watson, George, (ed.). *Biographia Literaria,* London: Dent & Sons, 1965.

Weinberg, Steven. *Dreams of a Final Theory.* New York: Pantheon Books, 1992.

Wesley, John. "The General Deliverance, Sermons on Several Occasions 523–531"https://
jacobjuncker.files.wordpress.com/2010/03/wesley-sermons-on-several-occasions.
pdf

Westacott, Emrys. "Soft Determinism Explained: Trying to reconcile free will and
Determinism." https://www.thoughtco.com/what-is-soft-determinism-2670666

Wiesel, Elie. *Night.* Translated by Marion Wiesel. New York: Hill and Wang, 1958.

———. *The Town Beyond the Wall.* Translated by Stephen Becker. London: Penguin
Random House, 1995.

———. *The Trial of God.* Translated by Marion Wiesel. New York: Schocken Books, 1995.

Wigner, Eugene. "The Unreasonable Effectiveness of Mathematics in the Natural
Sciences."*Communications in Pure and Applied Mathematics*, Vol. 13 (No. I) 1960.

Wenger, Mark. "Poetry and the Bible, An Introduction." www.academia.edu

Willard, Dallas. *The Divine Conspiracy.* New York: Harper Collins, 2014.

Wilson, Lyndsay. "Intelligence Testing: Criticisms." https://explorable.com/intelligence-
testing-criticisms

Wink, Walter. *The Powers That Be.* New York: Galilee Doubleday, 1999.

Wittgenstein, Ludwig. *Zettel (Slips of Paper).* Translated by Elizabeth Anscombe, ed. E.
Anscombe & G. H. von Wright, Oxford: Blackwell, 1967.

World Health Organization. "Gender." world+health+organization+gender&gs_lcrp

———. "Gender and Health." world+health+organization+gender+and+health&sca_esv

Wright, Christopher. *The Great Story and The Great Commission.* Grand Rapids, MI:
Baker Academic, 2023.

Wright, David F. "Homosexuals or Prostitutes? The Meaning of ἀρσενοκοῖται." https://
www.jstor.org/stable/1583059

Wright, C. H. H. ed. *The Writings of St. Patrick, The Apostle of Ireland.* Woking: Gresham
Press, 1874

Wright, N. T. "The Bible's Most Misunderstood Verse." https://time.com/6322429/bibles-
most-misunderstood-verse/

———. *The Day the Revolution Began: Rethinking the Meaning of Jesus's Crucifixion.*
London: SPCK, 2016.

———. *God and the Pandemic.* London: SPCK, 2020.

————. *The Resurrection of the Son of God*, London: SPCK, 2017.

————. *Simply Good News*. London: SPCK, 2015.

————. *Surprised by Hope*. London: SPCK, 2008.

Yoder, John Howard. *The Politics of Jesus*. Grand Rapids, MI: Eerdmans, 1972.

Zee, Len Vander. "The Holy Trinity: The Community of Love at the Heart of Reality." https://www.thebanner.org/features/2016/02/the-holy-trinity-the-community-of-love-at- the-heart-of-reality

Zowada, Matt. "What is Biblical Hermeneutics?" https://e360bible.org/blog/what-is-biblical-hermeneutics/

Milton Keynes UK
Ingram Content Group UK Ltd.
UKHW021332260924
448888UK00010B/212